Not a complete shambles

APPEARANCES CAN BE DECEPTIVE: A FRANK ACCOUNT OF A LIFE CENTRED ON A POWERFUL RELATIONSHIP WITH GOD

NIKKI ROLLINSON

Not a complete shambles

APPEARANCES CAN BE DECEPTIVE: A FRANK ACCOUNT OF A LIFE CENTRED ON A POWERFUL RELATIONSHIP WITH GOD

MEMOIRS

Cirencester

Published by Memoirs

25 Market Place, Cirencester, Gloucestershire, GL7 2NX
info@memoirsbooks.co.uk www.memoirspublishing.com

First published in England, March 2013

Book jacket design and photography Ray Lipscombe

ISBN 978-1-909544-46-8

Printed in England

This one is for you, baby.

INTRODUCTION

C'mon now, come take my hand;
on a magnifical journey we will go.

Don't be scared nor have a fear, for 'tis a place
you'll surely know! (anon)

This is a biographical autobiography; this is my real everlasting, never-ending life story. And God's too. **Primarily, and most importantly, it is the announcement of a celebration to come. This is the true meaning of life**. It is a frank account of my life, which is unremarkable at first glance, but I recommend you continue reading, persevere, because I also speak with no bullshit or pretence about the God I know and His personality and ways, and He might surprise you. In these End days God is calling in to His kingdom, and the celebration to come, those people who know deep down in their hearts that they know and believe in God but don't understand the Bible and don't want to attend a building/church or temple or whatever. Others haven't a clue who has the real truth. This is an announcement of things that are happening and will happen and includes people who cannot read this, those who are deprived or cannot speak English or the blind (or whatever the barrier might appear to be). The promise it holds is not restricted in any way. And basically, is a simply a witness; a written record.

I know the true ways of God and about faith and I definitely know the essential message He wants me to share. I look forward to showing you that He is like us and so much more. He has seen us all; He is watching over us and His holy Spirit is constantly at work, even though most people don't know His full purpose or value.

The DJ on the radio is playing 'the power of love, a force/voice from above, cleaning my soul... love with tongues of fire... make love your goal, love is the only treasure' (sung by Gabrielle Aplin). The lyrics convey very simply His love and peace towards us. Gabriel is an angel who is mentioned in the Bible and the singer's name Gabrielle, the female equivalent, makes the message more meaningful for me. God, the Father and Jesus Christ are speaking to mankind in one way or another constantly but unless we recognise His voice it can be difficult to know that He is, or They are, speaking.

I know His voice and it's been tough going; I have fought my battles (with the help and comfort and support of the holy Spirit) to hear Him clearly and get to the place where I can make this announcement and record my witness.

I am going to remain under extreme pressure until I finish the book, so I had better get on with it. Throughout the course of the book I have disrupted the flow of the narrative, typing in my thoughts, sometimes daily, as I have struggled to keep going. Hopefully you will see to some degree, the torment and the reality of what I have been through to do this. I understand, all too clearly, what it feels like to face a lost eternity and to feel alone and deserted, which makes me value God and the Lord, and the truth about Them is all the more precious. It also convinces me how right it is that I should share my understanding with you.

PART ONE

Job 19:21, 23 Have pity on me, have pity on me,
O ye my friends; for the hand of God hath touched
me. Oh that my words were now written!
Oh that they were printed in a book!

CHAPTER I

In the 1960s it was hip to be square, but in the 70s, when I was a teenager, to be square was to be straight; and we were far out, peace-loving, pot-smoking rebels. Language is a fascinating, ever-changing beast, which defines and moulds each generation. There is nothing new under the sun to this earth, but words can be manipulated to give every generation the illusion that it has defied convention. But that is all it is - an illusion. Today we can be well-bad, lush, radical, wot-eva!, all versions of square and straight and far out. Now I am a square peg being rammed into a round hole, in a frightened, disorientated, confused, insecure, straight world, scrambling to establish order and boundaries in an attempt to make sense of everything.

The only thing that actually makes sense (surprise!) is God's plan. I am a 'Jesus freak' of a different kind. His is the only way to find true order and liberty and prosperity and peace. There is hope; it's not over yet. Some might mock; others might think they've heard it all, but have they? See what you think; make your own decision. Freedom to choose is ours.

* * * * *

CHAPTER I

I have just been reminded that the brain is basically a big complicated computer and when a fuse blows it makes one hell of a mess. My brain finally blew a fuse a few months ago and I can confirm that this is very true. I almost completely lost the plot, went right off my chunk; I went to the brink and looked over into the black abyss of total madness and hell. My life is a life of contradiction and consistency and unpredictability. Makes no sense? Read the book and all will be revealed.

This could be classed as a 'self help' book, because eventually you might help yourself to the riches it contains but first you should see that God is looking on and listening and has the answers, and can provide the hope that politicians and our contemporaries cannot give. These are not empty promises. This is the truth. God cannot lie.

The eyes of the LORD run to and fro throughout the whole earth, to show Himself strong on the behalf of them whose heart is friendly toward Him.

(2 Chronicles 16:9)

This book is a based partly on my day-to-day life or walk with God. There are several messages that some will want to hear. The book is full of mystery and plenty of detective work is required. The great sex is also in there, but it's on a promise. I know some will want to hear what I have to say, as some people are looking for real peace of mind. This book will not be pc or poor (I can see that, can you? It depends on how you read/see/hear it and life with the God I know, *the* true God, is a lot like that) possibly not grammatically correct at all times, not what you know or expect, but He loves and uses words and language skilfully, so I might have to be pedantic. Realistically though it's essential that I 'keep it simple and real'. I can't guarantee from the onset that it will be a literary masterpiece (no shit Sherlock!), but I trust you will consider it with an open mind. 'Hi!'

* * * * *

My life does appear to be a complete shambles; it does seem I have fucked up big style. I have no visible security, no home of my own. Left to the system as it is, I am under the radar, a grey area. Without Him I would probably be on the street, or dead.

I have been to a dark place; at the time of writing I am in a dark place psychologically. I feel I am on the edge of madness. If I did not trust and know the Lord has a purpose for me in this I would truly believe I am losing my mind. It is not true but it certainly feels like it and it seems like all my choices in life have led me to a dead end and, in the twilight of my years, I am indeed virtually destitute and there are only two *visible* achievements I can be truly proud of. One is my son and the other is that I faced up to a wicked, deluded man who almost destroyed my life and those of my friends. He was another abuser disguised as a man of God and we were deceived. Most of us weren't idiots; we were simply looking for the truth and the will of God. It is incredible that none of us challenged him, but it was divine intention. He allowed us to be blinded and blinkered, to learn and understand what it means to be human and vulnerable. On the other hand we have also learned what it is to be eternal.

* * * * *

Words are part of my joy, and I constantly marvel at their impact on our lives. Time and numbers and physics also have their place and attraction and distinct relevance. This isn't primarily a book about my life in this life; it is to explain the reasons for my utter confidence that this is not the end but the true beginning.

Left to my own devices, unhindered by the doubts and cares and fears and reasonings and limitations of others, my preferred first name would be Joy, my middle name Optimism and my last name... I don't know my last name. Perhaps it is Yes (I can have everything I desire), which all adds up to a whole lot of Joy and contentment.

I am screwed up mentally at the moment partly because I am angry that I – WE - have been taken advantage of, partly because I have continued to listen to the criticisms and fears and doubts and worries of others instead of hanging on to what I know is true. I know the voice of the Lord and I know what I have seen. I've had visions; I know who I am. I know God and I needed to learn to not allow others to steal my confidence. In a sense I am fighting for my life; fighting to regain the life and the confidence and the joy and the peace that I know is mine, and which is available to everyone who can hear or see or feel Him.

I have come to understand that it is OK to be content and

to do everything I can to prevent anyone else from taking that and my other most valued and precious treasures away from me. My true and final place of contentment is in trusting one man; the only man who has all the answers and is totally faithful, in every respect. I know Him intimately in my heart and I have seen Him in a vision, once and only briefly. He, Jesus Christ, is my greatest and most constant friend. I see characteristics of Him daily in others but only He Himself has it all. I'm not a saddo, (or Catholic: I am a daughter of God, not a bride of Christ). I know He is real. I don't need physical proof. My life is evidence. This book is evidence. We are all evidence that God exists. Earth and the universe are evidence. There are scientists constantly searching for another explanation for how we came to be... why? Why do they need to find another reason for our existence? That is a great mystery to me. What do they hope to achieve? I am not a dumb fool, I still want understanding, starting with the basics. I have to understand as much as I can for your benefit. Understanding and information are power: power to be free from all constraints.

* * * * *

8th October 2012: Because some people do need convincing proof, I have had to seriously question my beliefs, now that I have effectively completed this work (the hardest part remains: staying positive, some tweaking here and there, editing, publishing, designing the cover etc. No worries at all, yeah right! I am a novice in the technological world).

My question to myself and to Him today is, 'Am I making empty promises, giving you guys false hopes?' My main reason for feeling this way is that I haven't any concrete proof or evidence, simply years of experience and trust. At this final hour it appears that He has forsaken me and not answered my most desired request (which is based on His promises to me). I feel utterly alone and plagued by doubt, at a time when I should be strong. I feel physically sick because my life does indeed look like a complete shambles, as if there is no hope, no positive way forward. 'Can I make one great last push and believe that they will catch my 'baby', this work? Will God meet me here and vindicate my trust and show Themselves victorious on my behalf?'

As always I am looking for a clear answer. At this point I tuned in to Andrew Marr's *History of the World (Part 3).* He explained that during the period of the Roman Empire, Christianity was growing and people wanted more than safety and entertainment and struggle. A young mother called Vibea Perpetua (whose faith puts me to shame) was waiting to die in defence of her belief; her testimony, by her own hand, is one of the few surviving records written by a woman from that period. Despite desperate pleas from her family to give up on her belief and save herself, she would not let go. This woman and thousands like her 'died' by the sword, suffered degradation and humiliation in defence of the truth, of the fact that 'death is swallowed up in Victory'. Death is not the end and failure, but the beginning of a new life and victory over death, the one inevitable thing in this life that we cannot prevent. I have to hold on, stand fast, be strong and finish this book as a mark of respect for Vibea Perpetua and all those like her, who have gone before and paid the ultimate price. God is real and He is here.

Unlike the Buddhists, who admirably have compassion and desire peace and limited humanitarian rights for all on Earth (in this life), the real way of God promises life and peace and prosperity for all eternity, forever, in a new incorruptible world. As you will see during the course of my cogitations, there have been times when I would have welcomed the ultimate Buddhist utopia of 'nothingness' but I would be selling myself and many others short if that was the real End, or rather beginning. The odds are very strongly in favour of the Truth, which this book celebrates. I am not holding a gun to anyone's head; we have our senses, we have free will, which costs nothing. Can I recommend that you exercise it?

I am fighting in a war against an unseen enemy. He is the unseen enemy of all mankind, but especially of anyone who knows anything of the truth and believes there is another life to come. It is a very lonely war if we have no one to unite with, if there is no comradeship, no support. The world is also battling against the tide of a very different circumstance. This war affects each of us in different ways: stress and money worries are compounded by unforeseen events and some money-grabbing bosses (not all but some), trampling over the little man to stay at the top, as this great spaceship we live on called Earth is sinking. (We are not aliens from another planet but Earth is very much like a huge living spaceship, built by God.)

These are the Last Days, and God's judgments against this enemy and all who support him are beginning in earnest. God has come out of His rest to mount His final defensive and show His overriding power against all who oppose Him and His followers. This is manifest in the onset of the signs prophesied by the Lord Jesus Christ, and John His disciple and Paul and Daniel the prophet and others. Those who have heard about these things might argue that there have always been wars and earthquakes and floods and times of famine and financial disasters, but these things are worldwide and not simply in specific places, and they are gaining momentum. The economic problems (which were also in evidence before the First and Second World Wars, for example) will not be resolved on this occasion. The populace will be crying out for someone to provide a solution, and that man is already in place; but he is not a saviour, he is a liar and a deceiver (another dictator) who is controlled by the enemy, which I have already mentioned. He has an ally in the form of a false prophet. Between them they will convince many that they have the answers to all the world's problems, financial and spiritual. This book has a message of hope for all those who are caught up in this battle and wish to share in God's ultimate victory.

* * * * *

'All is vanity', a Hebrew poet/preacher/king called Solomon once said. I have to disagree with this statement to a certain extent. For example, many people are genuinely kind and selflessly help others, with no suggestion of vanity or reward or payback. But this life on Earth is largely a vain show, and if I really let my own creative juices flow I would become vain about this book and it would possibly be total garbage or totally amazing, full of loving horny sex, but the ultimate satisfying sex, for those who desire it, will be worth waiting for. It was there in the beginning; for Adam and his Woman, just the two of them and no knowledge of right or wrong, no guilt. Their pleasure in each other was without bounds. Everything was theirs to explore and enjoy, but evidently there wasn't enough for the Woman (she was called Eve later). Adam clearly loved her but maybe he spent too much time talking to the animals instead of taking care of her needs, or perhaps it was the other way around? They knew there was knowledge of higher things to come, but they were not prepared, not ready to know such things (to partake of the tree of life). The woman was impatient (which comes as no surprise). Nothing much has changed, in all these years! But, Adam and his lady weren't entirely to blame; another force was at work, which implanted the thought that she was missing out; that their idyllic utopia in the protected Garden of Eden wasn't enough. If only she had been patient and waited until the time was right.

It might seem as if I am talking in riddles, which I am, to an extent, but all will be revealed and explained.

First, the serious stuff: I would definitely not want to limit the Holy Spirit, who isn't always serious, I must add; maybe you've already been introduced? He is the true Author of this book. Without Him, glory and attention would be taken away from the *only* Ones who truly deserve glory and praise. As I already said, God is '*The* Man'. Don't give up yet - you might be surprised. Surely a part of you wants to know what I have to say, even if you think you already know it all or don't want to hear because you think this is not for you? It's safe to keep reading. It's cool; no one is watching or judging. No judgment here. What have you got to lose, except for a few hours of your time reading something that genuinely has the potential to change your life forever? I regularly hear people who profess not to believe say 'Thank God' or 'Thank Christ' without thinking? Or they call out His name while they are having sex. Is it because they recognise it is an unearthly feeling? This isn't orgasmic but it is the lush, amazing truth, not the whole truth because that *will* take forever, but it is nothing except the truth.

While this is partly my story, I am also aware that the message it contains is from the Holy Spirit, on behalf of God and the Lord. I am informing you of this before you start criticising if you *are* a 'grammar snob' or maybe you feel that you have given up on God, or whatever. You might find this book changes your mind, unless you cannot get over these first hurdles. At the least, it should get you thinking; fill your thoughts with summat good! No insult intended. (Enjoy the parts that speak to you and ignore the rest, if you like. I was about to change the word *rest* to remainder but I have already used the correct word because this advice *is* to give you rest. If you wish to ignore the rest then that is entirely your choice. It has been a hard road to get here and I cannot/will not rest until this work is finished, so maybe spare a thought for me! There is a wonderful message, which I have heard and received, which I am compelled to share.

The Holy Bible* is the best representative of the Truth and

FOOTNOTE *Literal biblical quotations are taken from the King James Version (KJV), which is, I am told, the most pure translation from the Hebrew (Old Testament) and the Greek (New Testament). I would recommend The Amplified version of the Bible too, if you feel disposed to have a look for yourself.

it explains everything we need to know about God, as He really is (which is a statement that has offended a large chunk of the world's population, and my potential readers, already, but I highly recommend you give it a go, whatever your beliefs; this is not 'religion'; this is truth and real freedom). This is possibly the first hurdle to get over, or the second or the third; I can't answer that one for anyone else, but I can assure you it will answer some things that you yourself may have thought about, questions unanswered so far. Keeping to the main point, this book has a positive and encouraging message of hope, intended for all, though clearly some will not hear or want to listen. Some will immediately say, 'we have heard it all before, this is not new'. It's up to you, the choice is yours. The basic message is an old one but it does have a twist:

This is a true book about God and His humanity and Christianity; but not as we know it!

Some of you will already know Him very well, in this simple, uncomplicated way, though you might not even realise it. Doubtless you will have seen and heard Him and His angels moving around you or witnessed the influence of His power in the form of the Holy Spirit and not recognised that it is His voice. Perhaps this will jog your memory, remind you of dreams or confirm the signs. (Phil: Grieves to Joy - not coincidental. You recognised this much yourself.)

Be patient with me and persevere, the book *will* get better and better, along with my writing skills (we can live in hope), and my ability to type and use a laptop. The message it contains is worth your patience. Remember Eve!

CHAPTER 2

Before I go any further let me introduce myself: my name is actually Nicola Jayne and I am in my fifties. My experience of the world is largely limited to the last two years, but my experience on this Earth of the things which really count has been a life time, in fact it's actually many lifetimes. A couple of years ago (in September 2010) I was thrust out, headlong, in to an alien world (not, as I explained, from an entirely safe place) like a baby from the womb. I had a lovely home by the sea, which I loved and I believed, naively, that I was surrounded by friends, but much of it was a lie. It was an alien world to me because I was sheltered and loved as a child, but I was given confidence to recognise what is good and what isn't (I met my first paedophile at the age of five and stood up to him). Life as an adult has been a bit more complex.

Thankfully, I am *not* an alcoholic but I do enjoy a drink (or two) most days for pleasure and sometimes I enjoy too much more, like many do. I need to have a blow-out occasionally to let off steam, preferably when I can do some other stimulating activity such as dancing (I *love* to dance; I will dance again in the dances of those who make merry!), or going to a gig etc, combining exercise with fun – bonus - but these times are rare; (I can think of a better alternative but there is a drought on at the mo). Unfortunately, or perhaps that should be fortunately, such a blow-out inevitably means the following day is a goner.

Pubs with entertainment are an advantage, but the ideal pub/bar for me is one where I can talk about the Lord and share the truth and take in and enjoy some of the best spirit; the Holy Spirit. A hit from Him is the best high of all; I know, I have been there.

I am emotionally disabled because as a child I was encouraged to suck it in, to hold back my real feelings (even though I couldn't), and this is partly why I have had a breakdown; the mind can only take so much without release. I understand my parents' reasons and bear them no grudge. They are the best. They did their best. They taught me about love.

My parent's generation came stoically through the war years and this mantra of suppression and guilt was reinforced by the minister, also from that generation, who was in charge of our 'fellowship' (it makes me livid to think of it). This book is part of my therapy to empty myself of that anger. I've spent enough time feeling guilty about my life's choices. It's time to let go of the past and look forward to enjoying a present. I would imagine there are many others who crave this.

I like to stay skinny. I *need* to stay slim because I dislike myself too much if I am not. I look pretty fit on the outside but I'm probably not on the inside, although my blood results tell me I am. My mind seems like it's in a total mess, for reasons that will be made clear, but the good news is that spiritually I am well fit.

In my teens I enjoyed smoking hash/marijuana/weed and experimented with other recreational drugs, but I tried smoking weed again recently and found it no longer did anything for me; it's too potent and no fun, doesn't make me giggle any more and it only added to my problems. In an ideal world, none of us would need to experiment with, get high on or become addicted to anything harmful which appears to make life more interesting or bearable, but thank the Lord these things are available; more people would have lost their lives sooner without them but others have died because of them.

I smoke a few cigarettes a day (too many), depending on how stressed (or drunk or hyper or lonely) I am, but I do hope that I can cope again without this fairly enjoyable but unhealthy crutch one day (my lungs must have had enough, poor buggers). I certainly don't intend to worry about it because stress kills too and I would need more chocolate, and even though I *love* sex (I love to make love; my favourite addiction/sexercise and stress reliever by far, which you might find surprising because I have been sexually abused or taken for a fool) being celibate is not the perfect state of affairs. It is my choice, but hopefully someone will be good enough to change my mind before I get too old and knackered.

At this point in my life I struggle to see how I could ever feel safe enough to put myself in the hands of, or make the commitment to, another man. When I was younger I was very much into 'free loving' provided it was within my control, but even then it led to me having an STD, so now 'Wham bam, no thank you man'. I haven't closed my mind completely to fulfilling sex with another man, but a full-on relationship is another matter and unlikely but not off the table yet.

Trouble is, it would have to be someone very special and

maybe I am too old to find such a man; only the Lord knows if he exists. I am proficient at DIY and thankfully most of the time I know best which buttons to press.

I am beginning to be confident enough again to make choices about such things (smoking and sex; smoking hot sex would be preferable). Modern man is so repressed; it does my head in. I gotta have something... 'come on, give me a break guys!' I am speaking to those who criticise me for smoking, that is, especially friends who care and who are afraid I will get cancer or whatever. I am not making light of cancer when I say this, by the way, it is a most terrible thing, which has touched everyone's life in some form or another. My heart goes out to those who suffer in any way, but thankfully I know there is a better life to come.

I enjoy being around town or in the fresh air by the sea or in the hills; if it's not raining or I can easily dry out my things (mould can kill too (and it save lives); it stinks. This world is a potential death trap, decaying all the time. The echo system is finely balanced but there are disasters prophesied in the Bible which are starting to happen now which will significantly upset this balance. Perhaps I am a nut job?

A few good men who are trying to read this are possibly now saying, 'What *is* she going on about? Typical woman, all over the flaming place, rambling and gabbing on about one thing and then the next, all in one breath'. I know I sound like an idiot, but don't be deceived, I am most defiantly not. All will be revealed... well, almost all.

I would like to think that by the time I get to the end of the book I will have packed in smoking and resumed a healthy sex life. This is about the extent of my worldly or earthly ambition. My real sights are set much higher than that, but I do trust there will be sex in heaven and strongly believe there will be... because it can be rewarding! It was part of heaven on Earth for the first man, Adam, and his woman, in the beginning, so God approves of and encourages such sensual pleasures.

The Bible tells us (and by that I mean the Hebrew King David, or maybe Solomon, his son) 'The Lord takes no pleasure in the legs of man' (eg for walking, running or swimming, although He seems to encourage dancing!) so for me if I do exercise I have to enjoy it, it has to float my boat. Additionally, if it doesn't please Him (and I want to please Him; without that there is no real point to life), the things I do have to be enjoyable. I see no advantage in punishing my body, because most things from this life will count for nothing in the next. No medals from Him for running and jumping through hoops in this world or the next! It's really not necessary to overdo it (exercise in moderation keeps us fit and that's about it). For now, I must focus on Him and His will. If there is no eternal advantage or reward in doing *some* things I see no point in striving for them, so take comfort those of you who have lost your legs or are disabled, there will be no need to overdo the exercise regime in heaven anyway, as our bodies won't wear out or deteriorate. We will only have to do something if we enjoy it.

Look forward to being able to fly. I have put in a request for this ability, but there will undoubtedly be more interesting things to do that we don't yet know about. He has many surprises prepared for those who wait for Him. I have just realised we *will* fly because we will fly up to meet Him in the air when He comes for us. (I'm generally a bit slow on the uptake but hopefully not on that particular special occasion.)

I have no recognised earthly qualifications of any value: on paper I am practically a nobody, despised and ignored, but I have the experience of life that counts, especially in His sight, to get by, and I leave the rest to Him; the Lord has never let me down. He gives me what I need (and I have a hoofing girt angel by my side protecting me). He occasionally treats me to more, but for now I am on rations because I need to focus on doing this book. If He wasn't holding me down and restricting me I'd be off like a shot, out and about, spreading my wings. No cash flow, but that's a minor detail in the grand scheme of things. He has promised me some quality R&R later on; it will come, but not soon enough for my liking; no disrespect to Him, He definitely knows best! I know this, but I admit that I am struggling to accept it at the moment. Life is fucking tough going right now. He knows too that I am happy to combine my R&R with working for Him: I long to speak out about Him again, to those who want to hear.

I cannot abide being trapped indoors and would hate it if I couldn't see the sky. I panic a bit and almost fear it, but I know from experience that I would survive if I couldn't. Fear of 'things'; of God, of other people, of change in circumstances, or life or death and dying, or germs or loneliness – too often dominate our lives. There are very few people who can honestly say that they never worry about anything or are afraid of nothing. It is sad that fear is such a large feature of life today and it is certainly not what God intended for His creation. We should respect God, because He is God and our destiny is in His hands, but we should not be afraid of Him and that is why He wants us to know Him, because we generally fear the unknown... although that isn't *the* reason He wants us to get to know Him properly.

My first love is the Lord (not in a Catholic sense; I trust Him to take care of me better than anyone on this earth) but I also love all my friends and family to varying degrees, for different reasons. I love being by the sea but I really don't care if I am there or in the city or the countryside, as long as I can see the sky and the stars (and be within walking distance of the shops, I love shopping, especially if I have spare cash, and I love being among people). I like to feel the air around me (the rain and the cold annoy me and the wind drives me crazy, but I also love it because He brings the wind out of His treasure chest; it is a force or power of God that man can harness to some extent but which he cannot control. I love the Lord for that because there are some arrogant fuckers in the world, who think they are God.

I repeat myself a lot and unless I make lists I generally forget things. I love idioms and clichés. I love and respect words because they have power: power to inform and educate but sadly, power to destroy. It has taken me a long time to start typing for this very reason, among others. I have a responsibility to get this right but, as with all things in my life, I trust that He is in charge, ultimately, and my reason for getting this information out there is simple... He told me to!.. and the intention is to bring comfort and assurance and hope and certain joy to those who read it with an open heart and not too set in their ways.

CHAPTER TWO

I have told you nothing too unusual about myself so far, you are possibly thinking, but I am just giving you a sense of who I am, in my daily life; just an ordinary person, with a shitload of problems but extra-ordinary, God given, confidence and insight. (I hide it well!)

Financially I have been comfortable and I have also been virtually penniless; I am no different to anyone else.

I have been married twice; I had an eating disorder after the breakdown of my first marriage, a disorder which still bugs me occasionally to this day. I love good food but I wish I did not have to eat, as I sometimes repulse myself because the mirror tells me I look fat even though I am not overweight. But I must eat because I do actually like food and I had/have ME/chronic fatigue syndrome (food = energy), which is also why I hate being stuck indoors. I was forced to spend long weeks in bed and I cannot bear to be alone. I am lonely and yet I am not alone because He is with me, within me, but like many people I do need to be with others most of the time, otherwise I would go more doolally than I already am; I would prefer not be physically on my own, in fact, but I have to 'like it or lump it' for the moment, I'm sorry to say. I have to focus on this.

I was very ill and severely incapacitated for several years and had to use a wheelchair. I must credit my second ex for looking after me during that time and I know that this will also go in his favour when he eventually stands before the Lord. He stayed with me, even though he was reluctant to do so, and I expect he wonders what the fuck that was all about now we have gone our separate ways. The separation process was harsh, the Lord knows, but we were never meant to be forever. Thank you for your help, all the same, whatever spirit you did it in.

My eldest son committed suicide during that difficult time, when I was ill and unable to help him. (He is not lost because the Lord knows what drove him to it. He is stored in my heart and hardly a day goes by when I do not think of him). I have one other natural-born son, who truly is the best son a mum could hope for: I know I can trust him, He loves his Mum. (I ignore his faults; I'm not certain what they are, except he worries unnecessarily about everything, including me; I do my best to look for the best in everyone I know and meet, which could be a mistake sometimes, except nothing happens to me by chance and if anyone is mistaken in their intentions the Spirit steers or scares them away). My son has a beautiful, intelligent, patient, thoughtful, generous and loving partner, whom I love dearly, and they have given me a gorgeous, bright grandson, who spreads joy wherever he goes. He can be a monkey as well, but I really don't care about that because I love him so much for the joy and friendship we share.

I have a lovely, beautiful, gorgeous, strong, sexy, intelligent, tolerant and loving, caring 'diamond' of an unofficially-adopted daughter (that was expressed very awkwardly but it's true); she is one of the best. Chrissie and my mum are selfless and unselfish in extreme and I thank the Lord for protecting them and giving them wisdom in this (all my friends are very kind, I have to say). I cannot imagine life without Chrissie and her funny, high-spirited, lovely, edible children, or my other close friends and family. Forgive me, you lot, if it seems I have missed anyone out. (Hi Babsi, x thank you, Roland x, take care, Yuki x cheers Richard). I have simply run out of positive adjectives to use without consulting the dictionary. I cannot adequately put into words how I feel for you and what I see in you, and in some cases it is not expedient. (I know about stewardship, my 'best' friend, you know who you are!). The bottom line is I love you all, because there are qualities of Him in all of us. We are all special: not disabled/retarded 'special', although I do wonder at times – no place for PC. I want to have fun with the words because they are trying to do their own thing and go their own way, 'take the mick', make jokes and create double meanings constantly in my head. I might have to leave it alone for a bit if they don't pack it in. We are *all* special....'aah, bless' (I hate that platitude; it makes me want to chuck up!). I will apologise for all the I, I, I, I, I, eyes and the you you yous though. They are getting tedious, but thankfully we are nearly beyond this bit. I want to get to the good stuff.

* * * * *

The word *stewardship* is ringing in my head; it means basically not telling everyone everything about yourself, except what you want them to know. Stewardship is verging on a swear word to me. So is 'sorry' - we spend our lives being sorry and hiding things; *I* feel like I have spent my life being sorry and grateful to everyone. I sound bitter but I am really not, it's just that I have nearly always been dependent financially on others (so I have to be grateful) and it is wearing and embarrassing, even after a short time, for some of us and I have spent my life concealing who I really am. Stewardship is the word that was hammered home to us by the leader of the fellowship or cult that I was a member of for thirty years. He systematically abused and controlled all of us (adults, male and female, and our children), in different ways, to varying degrees, for His own satisfaction, and said we weren't to talk about it to anyone, otherwise we would be lost forever - control by fear.

Thankfully, I had a very happy, though sheltered, start to life (my parents and my grandparents were the stuff of every child's dreams), but I was physically bullied at school (to the point of mental breakdown, certainly blind panic, throughout my teens) and my eldest son suffered the same. Fortunately, with the help and co-operation of the school we were able to curb it and he had a couple of years of 'normality'. I miss that boy; he was my friend, he was misrepresented and targeted because he was 'different' too, poor love.

My first steady boyfriend was also a control freak, who dumped me for someone else when it suited him, but he did me a favour and I can guarantee he has regretted it since, at some point. But that relationship left me vulnerable and easy pickings for the abuse that was to come later.

I attended college but 'dropped out' to experience life after a couple of months. I could not see how I could be responsible for the education of young minds if I didn't have a broad experience of life myself (this was during a time when I did not yet know the Lord, as I do now). I have slept with quite a few blokes because I like men and I enjoy sex (I tried it with a woman but it is not my bag, not my flavour).

I have been married twice and both marriages were

influenced and largely destroyed by the guy in charge of the cult. I was basically raped (along with others) systematically for most of my adult life, by the cult leader, who was also married when the abuse began, and even though I didn't initially consent to it, he eventually wore me down and, I admit, I was totally persuaded that it was the right thing to do until my closest friend of that era (who was also abused by him) was committed to hospital for psychiatric observation and made a serious attempt to drown herself. I also witnessed him messing with Chrissie and grooming her beautiful innocent daughter. It was only then that I started to wake up to what was going on, to see the things that were happening all around me, and realised that it could never be what the Lord wanted. Slowly I began to look at everything that had gone on for all of us. There were some much more serious aspects to this, which I cannot discuss because others are involved, but the Lord knows and that is all that matters. That pile of crap will get his reward. I am reasonably certain that he has no outlet for his perversions anymore and trust the Lord on that one. The Lord will avenge and vindicate and compensate us.

As I said, I was a member of what I now know to be a cult. Two years ago my friends and I broke away from it (with the Lord's help) and this coincided or tied in with the final breakdown of my second marriage, when I also parted company with our beautiful home by the sea and the majority of my belongings, apart from a few sentimental items. Leaving my husband (and my home and most of my possessions) was not easy and it grieves me very much that our union didn't work out differently, but the relationship was strained for a long time for reasons I do not need to discuss. The damage is done. We both made our choices, and I know deep down that it was inevitable we would separate eventually, as neither of us was truly happy. My divorce process is ongoing; I just received a copy of his financial disclosure and it made me cry to read it because I realised that the final earthly ties to a man who I thought was my friend (we had our moments) were finally being broken. The money itself isn't significant, except for the fact that some of it is mine by rights; I need it; I am almost destitute. If you are reading this, my friend, be assured I have missed you and I sincerely wish that things had been different, but we cannot change that which is beyond our control. I bear you no ill feeling, despite the truths that had to be disclosed for the sake of the divorce and other things that only we know about. We have free will and we made our choices based on the information we had at the time: neither of us is to blame. We were led astray, conned and abused and deceived by a thoroughly evil man, who was himself deceived (largely led by his own mind and lusts). But it is my firm belief that ultimately, as with all things, the Lord was, and is, in control, and our hearts and intentions were honourable; if there is any shred of decency in us the Lord will recompense.

Oh yes... I must mention, I am also very easily distracted and flit about all over the place, if you hadn't already noticed.

Since breaking free from my old life I have been on a rollercoaster of experiences and emotions; massive highs and horrendous suicidal lows, to the point where at times I started to doubt that I/we had made the right choice, even though the thought of going back makes me feel physically sick. I have since learned that in my mind it is a place of safety and security because that is what I have known for so long. I am now out in the world and it is a scary place; it seems I do not have the right 'tools' to survive out here. I feel exposed, displaced. I have had counselling to detox and defrag my mind, to recalibrate, because it is as if I have been held hostage.

There are those who would say that if I know God so well, how come I needed therapy? Why would He allow these horrendous things to happen to someone He loves? This is allegedly a ministry of a sound mind and there have been several times when I too have seriously doubted my own sanity and the truth of all this. The only sound mind in my life has been God's mind in recent months, believe me. My problems are very, very real. As I said, I *am* like you, and I have needed to talk to a physical person face to face, who isn't emotionally connected to me, to get rid of all the psychological muck, the emotional toxins of my old life. It is no different to going to see a medical doctor for help. There is some positive stuff to come, by the way: this is real life, not TV soap or an American sitcom, although sometimes my life does feel very much like a cross between *East Enders, The middle* (a contemporary American sitcom) and a pantomime.

Checking out the reference to 'having a sound mind' in the Bible, I am encouraged: (2 Timothy 1:7-11) 'For *God* hath *not given us* the spirit of fear (the crap in my head hasn't come from the Lord); but of power (to get better, to overcome all these things), and of love (His love is constant), and of a sound mind'. This means we should be able to exercise self control, but in the full translation of the Greek words it also shows that sometimes it is necessary for the mind to protect and heal itself (when it blows a fuse) and become whole again and this ability/power is inbuilt. The mind is a wonderful thing, a finely-tuned computer, and given time and care it can repair itself. This process is accelerated if we can trust His word.

Especially encouraging for me is the following verse: 'Don't be ashamed therefore of the testimony of our Lord, nor of me His prisoner…' Paul, the guy who was writing to Timothy, knew what it felt like to be imprisoned or trapped by circumstance (he was actually in prison for a while) and by his thoughts. 'Don't be ashamed (the Lord is encouraging me here also) but be a partaker of the afflictions/ hardships of the gospel (partaker also means share with others, communicate these afflictions that have come as a consequence of following Him) according to the power of God: Who has saved us and called us with a holy calling (holy simply means blameless), not according to what we are able to do but according to His purpose and grace.' Everything is made manifest or clear because Jesus, the Lord, our King, our 'guvnor', is speaking out and I (like Paul and his mate Timothy) am sent to be a preacher and a teacher in this modern day. And (v12) this is why I suffer these things. Satan is none too pleased (which is a massive understatement and why I am being hammered) but I trust the Lord. He will strengthen me; I have already endured my darkest hour… I hope!

* * * * *

CHAPTER TWO

I have several messages to give to the world. The first one is from me and is purely personal and probably won't lift your spirits, or maybe it will, depending on which angle you are coming at it from: 'I am unemployed/broke/living on the charity of others, I am *NOT* stupid' (for some of us it is humiliating and restricting to not be independent financially but if your conscience is clear then fairy nuff, good on ya); 'I am ill, I am *not* stupid'; 'I am getting older, and a woman; I am *not* stupid.' There are more condescending insults like these, which I personally detest and which others will relate to and hate as much as I do. Frankly, I am sick of being treated like an imbecile, as if I am thick, as if I am weak and helpless, this does not help when you are trying to battle through. There are some selfish, thoughtless twats in the world. I already have enough to be angry about without them adding to it, but how are they to know? They do now perhaps.

I needed to get that one off my chest early on; I won't labour the point and there's no point ranting on (and I easily could! But I know I'm not perfect either). Most of you will know what I mean and have some sympathy. Everyone has a weak spot, a breaking point, unless you are a saint or lead a charmed life and have been well cared for and protected all your life. I have been cared for by people, at times, and I thank them sincerely for that, but I have also had to be humiliated and learn what it means to simply survive and still believe, and frankly, it stinks.

The other messages are from the Lord and they are the real messages (I have had visions: I have seen Him, I have seen my new home) and these messages also have several components, but they are far more meaningful and definitely uplifting because it is a Message from God, which I will share in due course (try not to groan at this point, sorry if I am boring you: this is not who I really am and as I already said, you might find yourself and be pleasantly surprised).

Few of the above descriptions truly define who I really am, for most of these things are temporary. I have had to endure some things that I would rather have avoided, but then I would not be able to relate to others' lives if that was the case. This life really is short and I totally believe in a better life to come (it wouldn't be fair for some of us otherwise, would it?) I believe emphatically and passionately that God and His Son, the Lord Jesus Christ, see all things and They are fair and just in all things, whether you can accept this or not. He is speaking to all, even those of different faiths, for we all are worshipping God. As Paul said (Acts 17) to the Greeks in Athens, 'Ye are too superstitious. For as I passed by, and considered your devotions, I found an altar with this inscription, To the Unknown God, whom therefore you ignorantly worship, Him I declare unto you' (calling them ignorant was not a 'put down' it was simply that the information they were given was not correct). 'God that made the world and all things therein... Lord of heaven and earth, lives not in temples made with hands... and has made of one blood all nations of men (we are all the same, we all bleed)... and has determined the times (timing is His)... and the bounds of our habitation (we are what we are, our life is what it is), so that we should seek Him, if we are searching for Him, and find Him, though He is not far away from every one of us.' Paul also revealed, as do I now, that 'He has appointed a day (a time), when He will judge the world in righteousness by that man (Jesus Christ)'. In a sense this is what He is doing now. He is responding to people who have good hearts and renewing a message of hope etc, and at the same time He is exposing those whom Jesus will judge for their wickedness and unbelief etc. I will explain properly what this is; it is definitely not what any religion today teaches (as far as I am aware, having some knowledge of most recognised 'religions'). Not many have a full understanding of the truth, but I acknowledge that there might be some others out there. I am not so vain.

I have been guided by God/the Lord for most of my life, but I have only recently really got to know Him as He really is, now that I am listening only for His voice and my mind is not clouded by man's interpretations of what He requires or who He is. As a child He was on my mind a lot and somehow I knew that separated from God I was not complete. I didn't try to analyse it; maybe I thought everyone felt like that. I never told anyone how I felt, but I was on fire for the Lord from a young age and I would always question and challenge anything I was told or taught about God which I felt conflicted with what I instinctively knew or understood about Him, with a child's mind (as my religious education teacher would surely confirm).

This confidence has been largely knocked out of me by life on earth and by small-minded people; I long to be that girl again. I mean that even as a child I had this feeling, this conviction, that when I was born and the cord was cut I had been separated from my best friend and my real family and that I had to find my way back to Him or meet up with Him somewhere in this life. I was sure that He was the One who would tell me the truth and guide me through this life. I strongly believe that children come from God and each child has that simple, pure knowledge of Him imprinted on their hard drive, if you like – the majority of us are inherently His children, His sons and daughters, it is just that some get separated off, away from Him and never find Him again, and some completely lose their way and become too damaged to return to Him, which is sad. I know He feels this too. There are others; unspoiled tribes in Brazil, for example, who cannot, even now, have heard the name Jesus Christ but they have a simple, uncomplicated faith in a higher power in their relationship with the jungle, their home. I have wondered if the part of our brain that isn't being used is where this knowledge of Him and our heritage is stored. It is not out of the question, it might simply be that we have closed our minds off and have forgotten how to access the information that is stored there and only the Holy Spirit Himself can enable us to access it. I certainly can bear witness to that, but it has taken a long time for me to free up my mind sufficiently to recognise this truth. Or perhaps that is only entirely true for some of us who are born to a particular work or calling for Him ('many are called, to Him, but few are chosen, for some specific work'). But, saying that, He has some purpose for all of us who acknowledge the divinity of His beloved Son (He cannot be restrained or limited by the limitations or constraints of this temporary life.)

However, this simple, childlike understanding and love for, and acceptance of, God is altered and coloured by what each individual child is taught, and our minds are cluttered with other things and with the many voices of this media-filled modern world, which squeeze God, our true Father's voice, out. To hear Him properly and to tune in to the information He has stored on our hard drives, we have to learn to filter out the many voices and noises and distractions of the world around us, including our own opinions. If you tune in and listen carefully, you start to recognise when He is speaking to you (He also uses the Bible a bit like a word search or text and if you ask Him something directly He will use the words contained in it to give you His reply, but He also speaks through lyrics and signs and nature – in so many different ways). Anyway, you will recognise His voice because He will speak to you in a way you can understand and you will see from what He says that He knows you and what you need to hear very well. Perhaps He already speaks to you, and I thank the Lord if He does; don't be ashamed of it; it is something definitely worth celebrating.

He is misrepresented and scorned and belittled at every turn and very few people actually *know* Him.

I am still every bit as passionate about the Lord, even though I am battle-weary and carry the deep psychological scars of a hard life, which to an outsider probably appeared to be idyllic. We all have our cross to bear, as they say, and like Jesus Himself and Paul the apostle and others, I bear the scars which prove it. (If we suffer *with Him* in this life in whatever measure, however, we shall also be glorified and rewarded with Him.)

Anyway, getting back to my story (so I can get the negative stuff out of the way and concentrate on the good stuff), in my later teens thoughts of the Lord were not as prominent. I had other things on my mind, too busy enjoying myself (I needed that time and I guess He knew that; He gave me that) but the desire to find Him was reignited while I was at college and the Lord eventually found me in civvy street. He hooked up with me again when I was 19, while I was dancing and singing in the chorus of a Christmas amateur dramatics production. He called to me and I heard that sweet voice that I had known so long ago and knew we were in business. Soon after that a mate, who I had not seen or had any contact with for a while, called at the flat I shared with my partner, handed me a Bible and said the Lord wanted to talk to me. I randomly opened it up to see the words 'Come near hither (here) that I might speak with you', telling me that He wanted to speak to me using the words in the Bible (like a form of texting basically). I did not physically hear His voice, but He spoke to me first through a song and the Holy Spirit touched me and opened my heart to let Him in. Then He provided a direct and precise way of communication that continues to this day.

What I didn't know, in the euphoria of that reunion, was that my initial joy would be fairly short lived (as is the case in life for the majority of us, with most things) and in fact it was the beginning of a difficult and sometimes treacherous and tedious road which I was about to walk with Him. Thankfully the advantages of walking this life *with* Them (our Father and His number one Son, Jesus Christ, and His Holy Spirit) far outweigh the hardships. As, I trust, you will see as the story unfolds. I do have a sense of humour and so does He, as I hope you will also see in due course, and the advantages far, far outweigh the disadvantages (but I can't deny that have found it hard going lately and difficult to hang on to this truth).

To continue with my CV: according to my calling from the Lord, I am a Watcher, which in Hebrew means someone who has their eyes open to see all things, an onlooker, like a guardian angel, basically a pair of eyes working for the Lord God on this earth. I am traveller (through time and travelling through this life), a prophet and a priest and a writer; a teacher, a guide and a daughter and a king. This is not bullshit or a con, nor the product of an overactive imagination; this is based on revelation, what He, God, has said to me. I know His voice and every role or position has a purpose in this life or the next. I have been walking with Him all my life, which precedes this life, and I have only learned a fraction of things there are to know about Him and the treasures He has prepared for those who learn to love Him. I have recently come out of a cult, so the previous two years have been a process of filtering the truth from the crap and retaining the core of my belief, which is that the Lord Jesus (the Messiah) has come and He will come again for those who acknowledge God, His and our Father.

The Lord has asked me to write a book and share some of my experience (ie give my testimony/witness), firstly to reveal and reignite the message(s) and secondly to show that God has rarely been well represented in living memory and sadly few people in this modern age actually know Him as He really is – as one of us. We are like Him and He truly is like us ordinary folk, and so much more! This book is mainly for those under seventy, because usually by this age we have made our choice, but there are those who are snatched from the fire at the end of their lives here on Earth. This is a message that He has given me for the world, for this generation and the generation to come. The intention is not to add to the Bible. Everything I have to say will doubtless have been recorded for posterity in, and have support and foundation in, that Word, even if I cannot quote exactly where (there is nothing new under the sun).

This is a celebration of God and His word (however you hear Him) and should provide evidence that it is relevant to us all in our lives today, but not, as I already explained, in a typically 'Christian' fashion or way. Another obstacle for some might be the fact that I am a woman. Historically prophets were predominantly men, but there were women like the prophetess Deborah and Miriam, Aaron's sister, to name a couple, and Mary Magdalene (she was despised because she was possessed by seven devils but Jesus cast them out of her). She was used to speak to the disciples after Jesus rose from the dead. He appeared to her first and He loved this woman very much. I know that the Lord loves me very much too and I also realise this is quite a statement to make, but it is true. I emphatically know who I am and my calling.

I must emphasise: this is not a new 'religion', I am not seeking to promote myself as a leader in any sense other than to reveal the simple, basic truth and show that we can all know Him and trust Him and have fellowship /friendship/communion with Him, as individuals. He is the ultimate teacher and friend.

CHAPTER TWO

★ ★ ★ ★ ★

A gypsy traveller told me while we were both enjoying a drink or three in the pub that he had taught himself to read. Because he wanted to know the truth about why we are here and where we go from here (the meaning of life), he had set about reading the Koran and the Holy Bible and several other religious or spiritual publications. Jesus Himself mixed it up with the down and outs and was good friends with the hated publicans (tax collectors back in the day) and 'sinners'. Based on what this traveller guy had read, he could not decide which one was telling the truth or how most of it related to his life. I invited him to ask me anything he liked and I said I would do my best to settle his mind, from my knowledge of God, from experience and from the truths contained in the Bible, a book I am very familiar with because it has been my primary lifeline and my support for many years.

When we had finished talking the man was clearly overjoyed, because I was able to explain things so that he could not deny I was speaking the truth; his questions had been answered simply, in a way he could relate to. In his obvious excitement, which he couldn't contain, he turned to his wife and said, 'She's a fuck-ing vicar!' So I guess my training was successful because he could see that I was a 'king'. I am such a kid at times, I am well in touch with my inner child, which is a basic, or rather essential, qualification, for seeing and knowing the Lord. As recorded in the Bible (Mark 10:15), Jesus (the Lord) said that in order to come to Him and the Father, we need to accept the kingdom of God and the truth about Him, in the same simplistic, trusting way that children accept and see things; and sometimes this involves being childish! I am not being irreverent. I suppose I am embarrassed that He has asked me to talk so openly about my life and reveal what I am, in His sight or opinion, to a bunch of people I have never met. For one thing it makes me sound like I've lost my mind and it also sounds as if I am bragging. But it is what it is. And I'm showing from the start that I don't take myself too seriously and He doesn't expect me to. Although I know He loves me and has said some wonderful things about me to my face and to others, my own opinion of myself is that I am a waste of space. I struggle with this daily. I despise myself.

The point is, however, the gypsy or traveller bloke could bear witness to the fact that I am a latter-day prophet (and my calling and work is of the Lord; I have fought many battles to hang on to and believe all of this and I have had years of practice, so don't be surprised or concerned if you too are struggling). I am an ordinary, down-to-earth woman who knows her stuff about the Lord and God, and in spite of the unusual setting, my own colourful vocabulary (my filthy gob) and my decidedly unvicarlike appearance, I was able to make things clear. I was whooping it up too inside, thanking the Lord. This man, who few people would notice and who very few people would respect (the lowest of the low, vermin, in the eyes of the world) could see past my appearance. He was oblivious to the circumstances and only heard the truth in what I had to say. He knew he had been touched by God. The Lord left me in no doubt that He and the Holy Spirit are with me, which was encouraging for me because I have been repressed and held down for years (by people) and I was taking a leap of faith in speaking out.

'Vicar' is not a title I would adopt (in fact I would never adopt any title other than Mrs (and Vicar and Mrs are certainly not in my job description) but thinking of me as a vicar was the only way that this uneducated, genuine man could make any sense of what he had heard. Bear with me, we are just starting to warm up. Hey, less of the 'she *is* a crazy old woman', I am very fit looking for my age and you hardly know me or Him, yet. Give it time, unless you think you have something better to do. We are considering eternity and what comes after this short, and often hard and miserable, life after all.

At this point, some might suggest that we are all the authors of our own destinies, that we are entirely formed by the influences around us and the choices we make. Some might say I have got what I deserve or asked for. My answer to that is - bollocks. For a start, on one level, my argument against this is that my parents never talked to me about God when I was very young, as far as I can recall, because my father was treated poorly by a repressed religious mother and he wanted me to be free of any such constraints. My mum and dad (my natural family) are loving people, who love the Lord, but we rarely talked about Him; He just *was*. I admit that if you feel inclined to read the Bible (which is basically a history book with hidden 'magical' extras) you will find parallels and similarities to my life (and your own). I find comfort in that fact, and to me this only confirms that the people in there are real, and therefore all the wonderful promises and prophesies are real also. Without a doubt the written Word of God, the Bible, has had a big influence on me and the person I am today, but more than that, I do not fear death. Do you?

On another level, in worldly terms I never set out to be unpopular, poor, unqualified; I simply took what life threw at me. I was a teenager, for fuck's sake, I was different, I had aspirations but no one to show me the way—and realistically there was only ever one way for me, but at the time I didn't know it. My own choices have not made me successful or popular, but I trust that I am exactly where I am supposed to be in the grand scheme of things, even though I am caught between a rock and a hard place.

Going to sleep, which is how we view death, would be a release for me because I see this world in all its darkest colours. I am weary of it and I rejoice to see His coming and the beginning of a stress-free, exciting new life. In many ways this new life has already started for me and I will explain what I mean by this later on.

* * * * *

In case you are wondering, another reason for writing this book is to show you, Reader, that you are not alone in your life's struggles. For one thing, God has had his eye on you the whole time. As you can surely see I (as a follower and believer) have had more than my fair share of suffering and pain and suchlike (sprinkled with some joy, thankfully); I am not 'holier than thou'. Nor am I a member of (love 'em) the 'happy-clappy; wishy –washy, Jesus loves you, doing their best but missing the mark', brigade. If you are 'one of them' I do firmly believe that in the main your hearts are in the right place, don't get me wrong, but if you have suffered at all in this life it is simply not realistic to smile and sing and praise the Lord all the time and expect God and the poor and hungry and homeless, to believe it is always genuine (and it pisses people off). We are taught to gather together and to praise Him but we cannot be religious about it; it has to be spontaneous and from the heart for God to hear. Respect, guys, you are having a go, you have a heart, and you are doing a cracking job, thank you... but maybe it's also time to take some time to consider your own eternal place and riches, His way. Plus, it's no help to those of us who are struggling or feel negative about ourselves, and about Him too at times make no mistake, for whatever reason, if all people can see is believers whoopin' it up, stuck in a rut, with no firm guarantees for future change and eternal prosperity.

I have no money to give. I am, regrettably, not in a position to offer practical help at this time; but I can confirm, however, from the outset, that the Lord (Jesus Christ, the firstborn Son of God) has seen our suffering and He does love mankind a great deal (let's face it He suffered and died for us!) and He has a very simple Last days' message to share, which, as I said already (God also repeats Himself a lot, just in case we miss things the first time) might surprise you when you hear it and give you genuine hope. In giving my witness I can be certain that I will upset some people (I generally do) but ultimately I have to trust and believe that it will bring encouragement and comfort to others who are looking for such direct and honest guidance and support and hope in their everyday lives, in these turbulent and uncertain times. (It is unlikely that I will be 'preaching' although I will give you the information that you need to draw the right conclusions and see and hear what you need to hear, which is that you know Him and He knows you and He is making you an offer). The deaf and the blind are also catered for in His plan.

The greatest obstacle to writing this book has been me, ie my lack of self belief or self confidence, because my confidence in my ability to hear Him has been undermined at every turn. Additionally, I had the problem of not knowing how to begin. This is a labour of love, which I was compelled to do (He asked me to write about Him, reveal the messages, to tell you my story and get it published) and therefore I have to trust in the confidence that He has given me, which is confidence in Him and not in myself or my own worldly capabilities, which are very limited. It was originally my belief that I was expected simply to keep a record of events. If he had told me I was going to do this, write a book, at the start, I'd have freaked right out. Until now I have led a fairly sheltered life and I am not exactly worldly wise; pretty naive, in fact... and worn out. The last two years have taken their toll more than anything else I have lived through. Friends imagine I am hard, made of tough, stern stuff, but I am not; most of the time I am bluffing it, holding on by the skin of my teeth. Except for when I am entirely alone with Him.

The other difficulty has been to exercise the self-control necessary to write in a way that is accessible or readable for everyone. It is tough because I love twisting and mucking around with words and I love to talk, especially about Him. I am trying, unsuccessfully it seems, to write as I speak and, to be myself with you. This does tend to alter according to the company I am in or the character of the person, or people, I am speaking with. I guess everyone does this to a certain extent and the Lord himself has many 'faces', otherwise He would never be able to relate to all the different colourful characters in the world. The word/the Bible talks of heavenly creatures/beings called Cherubims. They each have four faces, representing different aspects of God's involvement with mankind. Some of the more prominent and established churches/religions tend to target certain types of people, but God Himself is not like that. He can speak to any one or every one alike, on your level and it doesn't have to be in a building.

There is never any condescension intended on my part or His, nor is there any suggestion that I am acting a part, as will become clear as we progress. I just realised that I could possibly put this on one of those chat sites on the Web, as it's more like a long blog, if that's the right term. I've not joined that club yet. I'll see what happens! However, considering what I have just written I would be limiting His audience.

Radio 1 screams out: 'Praise the Lord!' Thanks for that, Fearne Cotton, thanks Kasabian; thank you and indeed Praise you Lord. Keep me focused, I have to stay focused and try and stick with it and not ramble on, or I will never finish the book. Or perhaps it is the Holy Spirit giving me encouragement by saying 'Praise the Lord, she's getting to grips with it; she's finally fucking twigged!'

I do have a problem staying focused and patience is another

weak spot, among other things. But there you go, such is life, none of us is entirely perfect in this life. (Muse) 'there's no justice in the world'; sorry mate, but I have to disagree; He, the Just One, Justice *is* here. 'Don't be afraid ...make a stand, stand up for what you believe, together we are invincible'; that's more like it. 'Use this chance to turn things around' Amen to that!'

'Whatever they say, my soul's unbreakable, together we are Invincible. Let's use this chance to turn things around!' Cheers guys.

I ask you not to reject this (although it's up to you, He never begs) simply because I am personally not such a great writer and because it is a book about God, or faith in God, based on what you already know, whatever you have been taught to believe or not to believe or think you do not want to know, because of commonly-accepted teachings and established religious doctrines, or for whatever reason. I am not intending to appear 'religious' because 'religion' implies bondage and control, and this is liberating ministry, revealing the truth in order to free us from the fear and the bondage and constraints of this life (to whatever degree this applies in your life). Eternity is full of good things and pleasures that we cannot even conceive of or imagine at this time. This is not my hope; this is a fact. (Join us.) 'Destroy this city of delusion' (Thanks again Muse: Black Holes and Revelations; more appropriate than you could have ever known. 'I am protected, not from trouble but, from hate'; praise the Lord for that one.)

The intention here is to guide, advise, maybe; encourage, definitely and defiantly, but mainly this account is basically and simply my witness, which is intended to bring peace to everyone of all beliefs and faiths and hopefully provide some serious consideration for unbelievers (He understands your reasons for rejecting Him) and agnostics (those who believe that these things are not our concern) and maybe even some atheists (those who deny or reject the idea that there is a supreme heavenly being and feel emphatically that we have no need for God in our lives). I ask that you join me on my journey (to use an over-used term) and form an opinion as we proceed, if you wish. More than anything it should speak to your heart and your soul; raise you from sleep. (I was going to say, as we go on, but hopefully I won't go on too much and bore you although you might possibly be bored already). But, as I was saying, I *am* easily distracted away from the point and my self-confidence is shot to buggery.

* * * * *

At this precise moment I have the many voices of past and present critics and advisers (myself included; we are our own worst enemy) ringing in my head: 'I am nobody, a failure, why am I still alive?; use correct grammar, mind your spelling, be careful what you say, do not offend, be PC, who do you think you are? You'll go to hell for this one, the Lord would never... blah de blah de blah. On and on and on... 'give me strength, please Lord!", this *does* go on and on, constantly trying to put me off, to prevent me from writing or typing. (See, I am doing it now!) I have to say it as it is and allow the Holy Spirit to guide me and prop me up. (Fuck!) Keep going, love.

Contrary to what many of you might believe, (and recognising that some people might not have heard much about Him before), the Holy Spirit is not well known and He is often far from appropriate or PC. I have seen Him at work and I believe/know we are like Him. Unfortunately, I appear to be one of those the Father has chosen to represent some of the most un-PC characteristics of God. I seem to spend my life upsetting people close to me and apologising for my very existence, almost. I am what I am (fuck all, nothing, in the flesh but I trust Him/know His voice etc), and while I accept this, others sometimes cannot accept me for what or who I am. They misunderstand me at almost every turn, so what hope is there that you will get it, dear Reader?

The Holy Spirit, the Spirit of Truth, always does things God's way, something that I cannot entirely claim to do; I have made my share of mistakes so I thank God *He* is gracious and patient. God's way is HIS way and is not our way; He doesn't think in the same way that man does, and yet, He is like us. How can this be so? It probably has something to do with the information stored on our other hard drive, the 'unused' part of our brain. But, keeping to the point, God can appear (note the word is 'appear' or seem) to be offensive (according to our/mankind's rules or opinions); He can be hard to swallow-and don't I know it! Pun definitely intended.

I was literally and repeatedly forced to take things in my mouth that repulsed me, believing that it was what the Lord required, that it was my 'sacrifice'; the sacrifice of my body, based on Hebrews 12:1 'present your bodies a living sacrifice'. This was not what the Lord wanted (His is the only major sacrifice necessary) but He allowed it to continue. Why? I believe it is because this is another example of daily life on earth, specifically of the abuse that young girls and women and children endure. I have experienced it first hand and therefore I understand the repercussions, the effect it has on the mind; it is devastating. It is repetitive rape and it is more common than I realised. As the recent revelations about the DJ Jimmy Savile have highlighted, sexual abuse is often hidden under a cloak of respectability and to outsiders the intentions of the abuser generally appear to be good.

I could have turned away from the Lord, from our Father, for allowing me to be deceived for so long. This life is a battle to get home and to see and hear Him. We have to be prepared to look beyond the offence; we have to really want it, we have to want to believe. It is not impossible to get over these obstacles, which the thoughts in our head, and our earthly education, and those who should know better, have put in the way. I can hear some of you breathing a sigh of relief and thinking, 'God and I do have something in common after all', He understands. He has seen and heard. And I can see others thumbing their noses. Some people do not want to hear what I have to say, my trust in Him is an offence. It's a nightmare being a pain in the butt to others when you don't intend to be; upsetting them with the things we say and do, even though we do not intend to hurt or upset anyone. Take my word for it, I have known my fair share of that bollocks. If I was texting you now, I would include a smiley face at this point.

I hope this book will confirm what some already believe and give them the confidence to turn to Him more often and talk about and share those beliefs more openly and without reservation or restriction. Or not. Either way is OK. You are probably wise to keep it to yourself (if you heard what I just said) but in spite of the negative reactions I have encountered I still love to talk about Him and the treasures to come. I know there are some great times to come.

Interestingly, the way of God is simple, yet He talks in riddles and parables a lot. This is a mystery to me too occasionally, when I forget what I know. We can only see and hear if we are given eyes and the ears. These things are not for those who would despise them. But there is no restraint or limits where God is concerned.

I realise that I am largely swimming against the tide here. Sadly, many religions or faiths are based on doctrines of fear towards God and rules, rules and more rules, because of ignorance and the corruption of the truth in order to serve the needs of those in charge. Frankly, God Himself initially provided a set of rules or laws for the children of Israel/the Jews to live by, but His law* was manipulated and corrupted by those in charge, mainly the Pharisees and the Sadducees, who don't believe in the Resurrection. What's that about? Not the resurrection, them not believing in it.

The Lord Jesus Christ (the anointed one, the One who has the light) came and died and went to hell and rose again, came back from the dead victorious (because He had done His Father's will and succeeded in making a way for us to be resurrected to a better place, to avoid death). The Law/the rules were scrapped and replaced by grace, kindness, love and understanding. We can see the modern-day equivalent of the

FOOTNOTE *There is a more to it than that, of course, the Law given to Moses was good, if it was done properly.

Pharisees and Sadducees at work in the Middle East even now and all around us. The fighting will stop, but not yet.

Rules are suffocating. We are made to conform constantly in our daily lives to what others expect of us, or what others believe is the true way of God, but in God's sight and plan He simply wants us to get to know Him and the astonishing power of Jesus' resurrection. There are no rules in His plan (of course, we still have to adhere to some earthly rules of this life otherwise there would be anarchy). What He means by this is He wants us to understand that this life is not a dead end and, simply through believing that Jesus is real and that He has risen from the dead, we can also believe that He has prepared a place for us and that we too will be raised from our final sleep, unless we are here when His Son comes again, in which case we will fly up to meet Him in the air/in the clouds. Belief in God is the *only* rule or stipulation.

I have heard talk of a 'Christian fellowship' in Canada which has excluded Christ/Jesus from their teachings. It might appear that I too am condoning this practice because I have said that the Lord has a place for all those of you who have good hearts but do not necessarily want to get to know Him. My answer to my critics in this respect is that time is short and I personally am not excluding the Lord Jesus; I am promoting Him and celebrating Him, but I can also acknowledge His astonishing and marvellous grace and His choice with regards to other people. This is His plan after all.

You may feel it is a sweeping generalisation to say that we are always expected to conform to man-made ideals and rules in some form or another in order to succeed, but in many cases it *is* true (this is certainly the case from my experience) but with God the only stipulation for reaching/attaining to/inheriting a better life in the next life is that we believe He exists.

* * * * *

Despite strong opposition to the truth, there are still many sincere and dedicated practising believers throughout the world. Some might mock those who believe in God and see them as weak people who need a crutch. My own dad was one of them until he faced certain death, which has a way of making you focus. Staring in fear at an unknown eternity is terrifying. But do not be deceived - a genuine calling or life of faith, following the Lord Jesus Christ, is bleeding tough and at times we are pushed to our very limits.

I need to take a minute to talk briefly again about fear and worry at this point. Fear is a very powerful tool or weapon and means of control and our greatest enemy, the Devil, Satan, uses fear very skilfully to his advantage and causes people to question why God, if He exists, allows people to suffer and they reject Him without waiting for the answer. Satan is the worst bully because he and his minions, the sons of God who fell with him, can appear to be angels of light and everything that is good, and they can manipulate people without their even realising.

It is always good to recognise an enemy. I recommend that you avoid talking to Satan though. Don't invite *him* in because he is very clever and he will rob you of everything (and he doesn't have horns so he is not easily recognised). We must not be foolish with these things and treat them lightly and ask for trouble. I certainly no longer have any fear in exposing him for the fake and bully that he really is, but I have learned from experience that I am protected, and I recognise him.

* * * * *

It is easy, when you know how, to tell the difference between the voice and tactics of the enemy and the voice and ways of God. We are our own worst enemies much of the time but if a person starts to think too much about the truth and the Lord then *the* enemy of mankind, the Devil/Satan, makes sure he fills our time and head with other things (erroneous beliefs, look no further than Hollywood and the movies for evidence of these things; success or hardship, he mixes it up) so that we have no time to think about God; he even had the nerve or the cheek to offer the Lord anything in the world that He could desire (the Father strengthened His Son and allowed Him to be tempted for forty days out in the wilderness with no food or water to prove to Satan that He couldn't be turned and to prove to us that He is to be trusted).

Satan was ultimately offering to make the Lord famous across the world, in His lifetime, if He would give His life with God up to worship him (the Devil). Satan knew that the Lord was vulnerable like us, because at that time He was a flesh and blood man with the same feelings and needs and cravings; Jesus was hungry and tired and worn out. He had to be, otherwise how could we ever believe that He understands what it is like to be a human being? He had to learn very quickly as a child and believe Who He was, the Messiah, the Son of God etc, and that eventually everyone would know His name (Satan knew what God had promised for Jesus, as did the Jews).

Jesus had not eaten for days and Satan tried to persuade Him time and time again to take his offer. This must have been a tempting short cut. But Jesus knew every detail of His Father's promises and He knew from experience that if He trusted His Father that this horrendous experience/temptation would stop eventually, which it did. Make no mistake, it takes discipline not to be distracted and resist such an offer when times are tough. Satan rarely offers people the world, as most people will settle for a lot less. The Lord as a man was a tough cookie, He was special; He *is* special and He had a very special job to do.

So, Satan meets us and uses distraction techniques to stop us thinking about God and is very persuasive and persistent. If we resist he can get vicious. I resisted and lost everything I possessed, along with my innocence, my health, and my eldest son and two husbands and he nearly had my mind (he is still trying to get that but he's not having it!). Satan would love it if I blamed God. We must understand, however, that it is God who will have the last word. He is the only one who has the power to cast us into hell. And some people will go to hell because they set out to defy God and do everything they can to ignore Him and try their best to piss Him off (the Lord can distinguish when this is blatant defiance and when it is a cry for help, trying to provoke a reaction). Others allow themselves to be manipulated by Satan away from the truth, because of greed or lust for power over others (mankind is so easily led).

But be assured, God is merciful and He can hear the smallest cry for help under any circumstances. He will save people from a lost eternity on their death bed, if in their hearts they are simply whispering or crying out to Him.

I must also explain that Satan can still walk around in heavenly realms and until recently he could still go into God's presence, into His courts (His heavenly Kingdom is a very real place, see for example the book of Job in the Bible, especially chapter 1). For a limited time Satan can walk and fly around the earth unseen but eventually, when his time is up, the Lord will throw him down into the very lower reaches of Hell (I will explain this more fully in a later chapter).

On the other hand the voice of God is quieter; His is a still small voice and it starts within us, in our conscience very often. Everyone knows, whether they like to accept it or not, that God exists. In the main we have to call to Him, except in some extreme circumstances when He steps in and saves people from sure destruction. Often He has to turn a blind eye when these individuals go off on a tangent and start following an erroneous religion and miss the truth, ignoring Jesus, because He doesn't look as good or appear convincing. Many people like mysticism and ritual, sadly. We have to ask Him, look for Him and eventually, in His time, when the time is right, He answers a genuine heart, answers our prayers or requests.

Occasionally He will respond immediately, as when people cry out to Him when a loved one is ill because He is compassionate and these individuals usually promise not to forget Him if He answers their prayers, and He still answers them even though He realises few keep this promise. God is not cruel, so if He doesn't answer then it is probably because the person who is ill suffers more if they live. The real test is, if He doesn't answer your prayers immediately... will you still believe?

The only control the Father actually retains for Himself is in respect of time and timing; He rarely interjects or interferes in any other respect. The times for things to happen in the lives of those who are His has to be perfect for everything to work properly, and waiting for Him, especially when we cannot see what is going on, can be a tough one - extremely wearing, and don't I know it!

Don't let what has happened to me put you off coming to Him. He is coming to you now, it is time to call you in. The hardships I have suffered have been for a purpose, to see if I truly believe enough to do this for a start, and without that I wouldn't have bothered. I have nothing much left to lose. It's not this tough for everyone and in some cases knowing Him will significantly improve your lot, if you've had a shit life so far. But, if we are fortunate enough to get to know Him well enough, if we are prepared to entrust our lives to Him, we are given promises of good things to come. Sometimes we have to hang on to these promises for some time, simply hoping that everything is within His control, because as you might know from your own experience in life, things can often get worse before they get better, and what we thought was the bottom line isn't the bottom line in actual fact.

However, I myself believe emphatically, I am fully persuaded, and can confirm that if we believe in and trust Him (even if at times we stop believing in Him because it just gets too tough) that ultimately everything will be OK for those who have trusted Him. His perfect will for all His creation on earth and in heaven will be accomplished, for His glory and praise. The majority of us (past and present and future) will be thanking Him, because what He has prepared is pretty special, trust me, or rather I must say, trust Him.

* * * * *

Regarding fear as a weapon, individuals also use fear to control and dominate others (I have experienced this first hand), whether it is a wife or husband or colleagues at work or other kids at school or church leaders; whole countries are ruled by fear by cruel dictators. We even control ourselves with it. To some extent it is not a bad thing, because without God and without fear man has no control. It is fear of the unknown that prevents total excess and mass destruction, and the same is true when we know the Lord, because it is the fear of letting Him down and losing Him that keeps us from destroying ourselves. We do have to recognise that because He is God He can do anything, so it is foolish to mock Him but safe to believe in Him.

Fear in one form or another dominates our lives but the Lord Jesus Christ came to free us from fear. The Bible tells us 'perfect love casts out fear' and it is only when we understand, even if only in a measure, His perfect and genuine love for us that we can stop being afraid. The problem is that it is very hard to be free from the influence of the fear in others, which can rock the boat and knock the strongest of us off balance at times. The main thing I now have learned (through bitter experience) is when to stop listening to others' opinions (and my own stupid thoughts) and it is only when I stop allowing their fear to control and rule my life and trust Him totally that I have peace with Him (see the central verse of the Bible Psalm 118:8 'It is better to trust the Lord than put confidence in man.' He is the only person who will never ever let us down, the only One who can save us from ourselves, from a crap life, from death; He is the only one with all the answers.)

He understands that I am vulnerable, as I am a woman and have been abused (because I am vulnerable and naive in many respects) and I make mistakes and I am a bloody idiot at times (the list is almost endless). He knows what we are and that we cannot be perfect in the flesh, as human beings. I can relax and be honest and totally myself around Him and it grieves me that I have to put on a face for other people, especially those who are closest to me. There are really only two people on earth with whom I can be completely myself, and they are both female.

Perfection can only be achieved by believing Him; believing that our sins and mistakes and weaknesses are forgiven and covered. Our humanity doesn't go away but He turns a blind eye, He doesn't care so long as we believe Him and therefore love Him. Basic integrity and a good heart are a good place to start. Even those who think they have sunk to the lowest pits (even some murderers) can turn to Him and find peace with Him and within themselves. Achieving perfect peace with others is a harder call because it is basic human nature to find something to criticise. For some reason we find it harder to overlook and forgive one another's faults. It is so much more encouraging and uplifting to find something positive and encouraging to say. Unfortunately there are some who take advantage of an open heart, but the Lord doesn't allow them to fool me for too long.

Other people are afraid to be seen in the wrong light. They cannot bear to think that they might be thought of as being tight with money or withholding kindness of any description from others. This is why registered charities succeed and businesses can fail. Banks are another matter - we all know why they keep going but that's not my concern. It is called 'good works' and these works are nearly always done to convince others or ourselves that we are good people. Ultimately at the bottom of it there is also the insurance factor: 'if God is watching, or if God really does exist then surely He will take this into account.' This attitude has been nurtured by some recognised Churches to put bums on seats and money in coffers. What most people cannot grasp is that all that God, the Father, requires from us, all that we have to do, is believe that God exists and for a bonus, that Jesus is the first Son of God. He wasn't simply just another prophet; He actually came (and paid the ultimate price, the only sacrifice that counts in God's sight) to pave the way for us to heaven and to a better life to come. It is as simple as that.

Knowing this, and believing in Him with a genuine, honest heart, comes first (honesty with God, the Father, doesn't mean we always have to be honest with everyone else). If we then feel we want to help others because it makes for a better life in this world then fair enough, but it means more to God, the Father, if we believe in His Son. Be assured however that if you simply have a good heart, even if it is well hidden, God has seen you and is interested in you.

There is a more basic level of salvation. This message

contains something new, which will no doubt be controversial and attract some criticism from the 'purists'. I know I have talked a great deal about the Lord (Jesus Christ) because I know Him as our Saviour, (in more ways than one, without Him I would be lost) and you might assume that the message He now has to give is only for those who believe in Him now (and you might also think that heaven sounds like a very boring place, but that is a lie from the pit). I can explain that the first and most significant message is that these are the End days, we are approaching the time of His coming: **HE IS COMING. He will come down from heaven to meet us in the clouds.** In these final hours of the history of the World, He is saying that He sees a good heart and, SO POWERFUL AND WONDERFUL IS HIS GRACE and love for the people that He created; He is now calling those who have a good heart and giving you the assurance that you will be welcomed into His Kingdom, in Heaven. God the Father has broken His Own rule, which was that since His Son first came to earth, as Jesus, and was murdered by those Jews (His original chosen people) who took offence at His decidedly un-god-like, un-Messiah-like appearance and background and teaching, that after He rose again from the dead, the *only* way to get to heaven was to believe in Jesus Christ, His Son. But the Father has revealed that time is short and it is now time to call people from the highways and byways, the back streets, ordinary men and women, those who have slipped under the radar, with all their faults and problems, whatever income bracket, whatever their background, and invite you to His home, His Kingdom, to His party, His celebration, for He (the Lord Jesus Christ Himself) is coming for us soon. So, even though it isn't absolutely necessary, you might like to take this opportunity to get acquainted with the host, get to know Him a bit, just by continuing to read this and saying 'Hi' to Him yourself, while there is still time.

I can explain for the 'purists'- even though I do not have to: Originally the children of Israel (the Jews) were the only ones who were destined to make it to heaven (the rule or law then was the Ten Commandments, which were given to the Children of Israel to protect them and enable them to stay focussed and on track). After the majority of the Jews rejected Jesus as their Messiah, the rule changed and faith was opened to all and the condition for getting to heaven was through belief in the Lord Jesus Christ, (as I have clarified for those of you who did not yet know). In these last days God, in His infinite wisdom, has chosen to show me that now's the time to call in those of you simply with genuinely good hearts (and it is there in the Bible), if you can believe it. It is His prerogative; He can do as He likes and reveal things to whomsoever He chooses. I, for one, am not going to challenge Him on it.

Getting back to the joy of this event, His coming, we will hear a sound like the sound of a trumpet and the Lord Jesus Christ will appear in the clouds. In the blink of an eye we will be changed and we will fly up to meet Him in the air and He will take us to our 'long home', a much better place prepared for each of us forever, for all eternity. Those people who have already died, or gone to sleep, I am assured, have already woken up in heaven, with their new body. This is a surprise to me because the Bible tells us that they would wake up and their spirit would rise first and that we would all meet in the air with Him. I cannot explain why this has changed, or if it actually has changed. Perhaps it is how it is expressed or my understanding of the account that calls me to question it.

I have only just noticed that Paul makes a distinction between those who *sleep in Jesus* and the *dead in Christ*. (See 1 Thessalonians 4 for details.) I understand now that this possibly means that He will bring those who were asleep to get those of us who are still here. One amazing reunion! I guess they won't meet Him till that day either. I am inclined to believe that *the dead in Christ* are those who have known and rejected Him (and who will have to answer to God for their deeds) who are kept in a mass grave in another dimension... all will be made clear when the trumpet sounds and He appears. I don't have all the answers. I can wait.

Don't be put off by that word 'eternity' (younger people shouldn't find it so difficult to grasp) but it can seem a bit daunting because some of us are pretty knackered and the thought of life going on and on forever is just too much to handle even though it is going to be different and amazing. We simply cannot grasp it with our limited, earth-bound minds, but we will be changed, given a renewed incorruptible body and a new mind. We will be given a new body, which will not get old or decay but somehow will look the same. We will understand and be able to handle it, and it will be incredible and pain free; no more bad stuff, no more tears, no more worries. With the sight we will have then, we will have no concept of whether someone is attractive or unattractive in the way we judge people by their looks or outward appearance.

This is an earthly limitation/fault and one that was in the original heaven too (as you will see in a while).

I use the term 'soon' very lightly because I have learned that His 'soon' and mine are two very different things, but He has assured me and my friends that it will not be very long; in my lifetime (and I am 54, so you do the maths). Realistically it could be another thirty years, but the signs are that it will be much, much sooner. He is asking those of you who can hear His call now to look up, be expectant and not be afraid. He has been quite insistent; the time is rapidly approaching. I don't have an actual date, as the timing for this main event in His calendar for this earth is a closely guarded secret; only the Father Himself knows the exact date and I believe that's because He wants to surprise us all. The Jews (the children/family of a man called Israel), who were originally the only people chosen to know and approach Him (ie God, Jehovah; The King of kings, Lord of Lords etc) are in for a shock because they are still waiting for His Son's, their Messiah's, first coming, but their experience and what is going to happen for them is another story, which I will touch on later.

* * * * *

I am beginning to see that this book is going to evolve and take on a life of its own, so perhaps there is a slender argument for evolution (ha! Right!... give me a break!) With tongue in cheek, I take the piss because I cannot even entertain the concept of evolution or for that matter, one big bang; they are just too ridiculous... if you really think about it.

I believe Creationists believe in creation *and* evolution. Scientists do not say we evolved from apes, they say we evolved from ape-like ancestors, some of which evolved into humans, some into apes. There might well have been some ape like people in the beginning - there are still a few knocking about even now! But seriously, it is my guess that they were created and introduced by Satan/the devil; as were dinosaurs. These were *not* part of God's original creation. As I will explain later on, Satan will stop at nothing to destroy and undermine what God intended.

Regarding the Big bang, it is only a theory; it has not been categorically proven. Some scientists now agree that a big bang was not responsible for the universe coming into existence and other scientists agree that some form of big bang took place. I also agree there might well have been some crashing and banging involved, but the bottom line is we were created by God and He made the earth. Scientists are persistently making new discoveries which counteract and contradict previous discoveries, but God's word is constant regarding how the world etc was made.

God anticipated this need to find another way (and frankly He made us intelligent beings) but He is way ahead of man. Interestingly, after the Flood in Noah's time everyone spoke the same language and they built the equivalent of the huge tower blocks of today, which reached in to the clouds, suggesting that this was intended to be some sort of observatory. The Lord saw what they had done and mixed up the language and scattered everyone because He realised that mankind would destroy itself again and get away from the truth, if He didn't intervene. The simple truth can get pushed out if we start questioning everything and my beef is basically with those who want to find another answer, another way, in order to prove that God does not exist. The Bible tells us that in the End days it will be the same as in the days of Noah, in many ways; e.g. acute self indulgence and abuse of mankind; and today a large proportion of the world speaks English or Spanish and the internet has eradicated many barriers. These are simply signs that these are the last days and the world is spiralling into destruction and God is beginning to intervene once again.

Of course particles are also in His creation (particle theories), but He is a better scientist than any of us will ever be, so why not believe in the truth? Why do some people feel the need to prove God wrong? Why not learn from the Master, understand everything; let Him explain. 'What is the point, if there is nothing after this, nothing better to come? Where is it leading us? What comes next... nothingness? Really? Or would we really want to live forever in this fallible form?

I will include the observation here for any critics, simply because I can, that in my humble opinion we should differentiate between evolving and adapting. Clearly our cells have adapted to cope with the ever- increasing number of viruses, which are also mutating. The human body was set up by God in the beginning to do this. The basic building blocks, our DNA, remain the same. I marvel that some scientists can understand such an incredible piece of machinery and believe that anything relating to this intricate set up was random, or an accident.

I am told that many scientists do credit God as the ultimate higher power and praise the Lord for that. I had a friend who was a believer and who became a scientist, and I have to say his faith was more pure and simple before he became a scientist. Intelligence or the need to know too much about this earth and the rest of creation can be a hindrance to faith. I find it all fascinating but I am thankful that I can keep it simple. If anyone gets bogged down with these earthly matters then they will have missed the point and the message that He is coming and is making an amazing, wonderful, exciting, calm, problem and pain free new place for some of us to live. And the message is for those who want to hear.

It is provocative to mock, I suppose, and occasionally people use this humour with me (they take the piss) and I don't like it, I can't shrug it off, especially when I am feeling particularly fragile or sensitive, which I must say, has been most of the time in recent months, due to my mental meltdown (see below). I have had to accept that He hasn't chosen me because I am the strongest or the greatest but because I am the weakest.

One of the major reasons for sharing my story is to show God, as I have known Him, as a very 'human', or humane, character, although I use this term loosely because He is God and He has abilities and powers that we cannot access (much better than any blockbuster movie representation).

He doesn't need me or anyone else to do anything for Him but He wants us to join Him in His works (and share in the happiness and fun and rewards to come). He has asked me to do this one final thing and even though I battle with it every day, I am driven to continue, in this I have no choice; and it is my only place of real peace and solace. As I read back over what I have typed already I wonder who the woman is that is writing it. I do not recognise her as myself because she is so positive in her trust in Them (in God).

Miracles most definitely do happen, but at this time I do not yet have the ability or power to perform miracles such as healing, or of any useful description. One time when I was ill with ME I couldn't get out to buy my husband anything for his birthday and I didn't have any money of my own, as such, anyway. I decided to make a cake but only had about a dessert spoonful of icing left in the packet. I asked the Lord to make it stretch. To my utter surprise I mixed it with some butter and spread several layers over the top and around the sides and there was still some remaining in the bowl, which I put in the freezer because I couldn't bear to throw it away. It was totally bloody exciting. I guess He was just showing me that He loves me and if He needed me to do a miracle He does hear me and honours my requests.

I am waiting for another much bigger miracle that He has promised and He is waiting for His time and I am struggling to hold on to my sanity as He waits (for whatever reason), but I know He ultimately won't let me go or let me down. He hasn't called me to make a fool of me. I am not in a hurry to be given such power, as I would be under pressure to use it. Writing the book is sufficient in my estimation but He might have other ideas. See what happens!

For the time being this book, and what I am given to say in it, is His work for me. I do not intend to be flippant or approach it lightly, although I am free to show my playful side, because I am representing the King, The Ruler and Creator of all things, who definitely has a sense of humour, but making me wait for the personal thing He has promised is *not* funny. And I am in no hurry to perform miracles; I would get no peace, if it was common knowledge.

* * * * *

You will see, I trust, from what has been said so far, that He understands modern life as we know it (in its many different forms; nothing shocks or surprises Him; there is nothing new under the sun, as King Solomon said) and, partly through my own experience of life, there is a revelation of God, which begins and will end with the glorification of His Word, His wonderful beloved Son, the Lord Jesus Christ and the incredible gift of life that He brought, will be revealed in its dazzling fullness when He comes. Eventually the Son, the Lord, will hand this completed work, which started in the beginning, when the earth was first made or created, over to His and our Father and our new life in heaven will continue to grow and our joy will increase, as we enjoy living with His family, as His family. And it won't only involve lying around on clouds and playing harps, I can assure you (if you fancy a bit of that it might not be out of the question). We are told that we do not have a clue about what He has actually prepared for us, but He has many wonderful surprises prepared and waiting. I have no doubt that He will satisfy our every desire and dream and more and we will be praising Him forever for

His great goodness. I feel I cannot wait, but I have to. I need to crack on with this first.

This is not simply an account of my life. It is my testimony or witness and a celebration of the truth that few people are aware of, or appreciate (I am not so vain as to claim that I am the only one, but it has fallen on me to speak to you at this time).

For some people God is the last resort, the One they turn to only in desperation, in an hour of desperate need, but, thank God, there are also people everywhere who hear Him speaking to them daily, weekly, in many different ways. I hope to show that He is one of us, He is like us; He is all things to all men and women and children; He is not a demanding tyrant to be feared; He is real and living and He really did make us (create us) to be like Himself ('in His own image', so He must look like us for a start, even though the Father Himself is a Spirit, or not a physical being as we are). The Lord Jesus, however, has a body like ours, but it is now incorruptible. God the Father will live in us; He can live in us now, His Spirit joins our soul/spirit within us if we believe. This is basically what being 'born again' is about.

The Father made us to be His Son's friends. He also desires to communicate with us, to have fellowship with us, to regularly hang out with us. He is not unattainable and perfect (as we might view holiness and perfection). Every one of us is invited to get to know Him, to hear Him, but most of all He wants us to relax and know that He expects everyone to stop worrying because He is in charge of everything ultimately and He wants nothing from you, other than that you believe that He does truly exist. He wants us to be at peace with Him. He knows exactly what is going on, at all times, on earth and in heavenly realms or dimensions. This is His creation and His work, for His purposes, and there are some people in authority in established churches/religions who will be called to account for their actions, make no mistake. He certainly knows us (nothing is hidden from Him) and in these turbulent and uncertain times you just might like to continue to listen to what He has to say. The choice is yours.

CHAPTER 3

'We are not prisoners. Traps and snares are set about us, but there is nothing that should intimidate or worry us.

We are set down in this life and we have, over thousands of years of accommodation, become so like (Them).

That which we hold still, we are. But, through unhappy mimicry we are scarcely to be distinguished from all who surround us.

'But we are not prisoners. We are free!' (Rilke, We are not prisoners)

* * * * *

In recent weeks I have been very close to total mental collapse (and I'm not out of the woods yet). To any onlooker my life preceding this time probably looked idyllic, but in actual fact it was a huge lie. My circumstances now are hardly sweet and conventional and not actually on the face of it, at first glance, a glowing recommendation for what I am sharing with you, but my experience is sound.

I have very few outstandingly happy memories, or at least they are buried under the mountain of my present despair. This is my lowest point to date - I think. I am deliberately interjecting the narrative, showing the contrast between my daily battle with my critical and self-deprecating earthly/fleshly mind and my positive spiritual conviction and belief in Him. When He comes and we go to live with Him forever all the bad stuff and the struggles of this life will be utterly forgotten, praise the Lord. I can guarantee that if you bear with me and continue reading, that this book will change your perception of a very emotive subject, or strengthen any existing opinions or beliefs that you may or may not already have. The saying goes 'never talk about politics or religion' but this is not about 'religion', it is about real, alive and living faith. I am not afraid to speak up about my beliefs because, although on the one hand they are about endurance and patience and a certain amount of pressure and suffering, they are much more than this; they are a message of grace and love and peace and hope and about promises that He has made to individuals and to mankind throughout centuries, promises which He will keep.

Let's face it, not many people have a trouble free life here. If I were to come to you, as a believer, and tell you that my life has been a complete bed of roses you would surely think I was lying or that we have nothing in common. If I am correct in my beliefs (and make no mistake, I am fully persuaded that speaking to you is what the Lord wants me to do despite the opinions of some who would challenge me on this), your own personal understanding of God and life and our reasons for existing, which is basically that we should know Him and, by extension, who we are, should be enriched and without a doubt show you that the common perceptions based on what we are taught or can see or are led to believe, have become distorted with the passing of time. Some will reject what I have to say immediately on principle; others will be looking for answers and will value this honest and human and simple explanation of things which undoubtedly play on everyone's mind at some point in their life.

I thank God, our heavenly Father and His wonderful Son the Lord Jesus Christ and His Holy Spirit for enabling me to do this, and without sounding too much like I'm giving a speech at an award ceremony, I must genuinely also thank my friends and family who have supported me and stuck by me (just about!); for their patience and love and kindness and generosity to me during an extraordinarily difficult time, in acknowledgment of their own battle to hold on to their faith and, on occasions, to accept that I have not lost my f...ing mind (or that some of them have not lost their own way or minds also) and that I/we have made the right choices, despite how contrary and thoroughly messed up things have appeared sometimes. 'Complete Shambles' was the title one of my newest friends, who has no real idea what I am writing about, suggested and, big man, as you can see I have incorporated it, so I owe you a drink when this gets into print and in circulation.

I came across the piece of paper where I had recorded this title option. I had written 'Complete Shambles' and above it I had also had made a note of a comment I heard during a film, 'God doesn't build in straight lines'. I had asked, 'is this true?' A complete shambles is the very opposite of neat straight lines, so I guess He doesn't. This explains a very basic thing about God. As far as I can see in nature, in His creation, the Lord Himself did not build in straight lines, there are always curves and shapes and His will is like that. At times it can seem like it is all a complete shambles but He has set everything up to work properly (with several curve balls) if we do not interfere with it, which is easier said than done.

In my darkest hour, when it has been most difficult for me to hang on (for *us* to hang on!) it has been incredible to me to realise that some still care. There are others who doubt and oppose me who should know better; I pray God that He would forgive their ignorance. I do not understand why they feel they know better than me; perhaps it is because past experience has taught us to doubt and challenge everyone. This has been an incredibly difficult path for us all to walk, in order to get to the place where these things can be revealed and God's message can be shared with all who are ready to hear.

A close friend commented only a couple of days ago about the Lord's teachings about false prophets, who will be prolific in the end days. It seemed that the suggestion was that I am teaching false doctrines. It grieves me that any of us who survived the cult should seek to unite and support one another against me or anyone else, for that matter. This friend's understanding appears to be limited or restricted in some respects, and that may not be his choice; it might well be that the Lord is protecting him. If it is his choice I do not criticise him for that. Hey, we all have to do what we have to do. We are not all the same. I understand he feels I have gone feral. Time and events will tell.

This is my testimony; the record of my personal battle which God, our Father, has permitted so that I too understand the basic challenges and hardships, which are a part of everyday life and also of the joys of knowing Him, more importantly.

I am fighting now to continue writing as once more my own mocking rings in my ears. 'I sound like a twat', 'who the f.... do I think I am?' Same old, same old incessant annoying crap intended to stop me speaking out but, as always, I shall persevere. (Do not be offended by my language dear reader; the middle class elderly and some Christians might suck in or 'tut tut'). This is not bullshit in any form, this is the truth. If you are struggling with this, can I just ask you to imagine Jesus and His disciples for one moment? He was conceived outside marriage, His earthly 'dad' was a carpenter, He lived in a dump of a place, some of His disciples were rough fishermen (for the moment I forget what the others did, except for Luke, who was a doctor), some were more educated than others but they were all plain ordinary earthy guys; not particularly eloquent or always socially acceptable, probably rarely. The Lord Himself came from Nazareth, which at the time was the pits, a real dump of a place. One of His disciples, James, advised us not to offend others (wind one another up) with words, but he was talking about not being nasty to each other, and running one another down. He wasn't talking about swearing or letting your hair down and having a laugh and a joke, while having a drink! Life is tough enough as it is and if we are blessed enough to have friends and/or family the last thing we should do is constantly police and criticise one another and make life more difficult for each other. It is the horrible shit that comes straight out of a wicked heart which separates friends, and this is what God hates, not swear words. Sometimes crude words are the most descriptive, but I will do my best to keep the swearing to a minimum for the sake of those readers who do find it offensive. Sometimes they cannot be avoided, because they are often the most powerful and expressive words to use. In my estimation it seems ridiculous that these words aren't acceptable to everyone. It's snobby bullshit.

Let me also make it clear; God doesn't expect us to like everyone. There are some people who I cannot like (but I do love) and others are blatantly wicked. From a personal viewpoint, there are some people who have affected my own life very negatively, whom I dislike with a passion (for justifiable reasons), and some of my close friends almost drive me insane at times. I certainly annoy them. It *is* a miracle in itself that we are still close friends: there's not many of us left, but I still love most of 'em and some still love me, I hope, although I can't be certain because they are not speaking to me!

My point is, however, that 'swear words' are nothing, they are just words. Perhaps you have never really suffered or eaten dirt - I thank God on your behalf, if that is the case - or perhaps you are simply more intelligent and refined, and there is nothing wrong with that either. Don't get me wrong, I too have my more refined moments. I also like to relax and be completely myself, but those times are rare, as is the case for many others too, I would assume. I have my 'trashy' side, which I love but can't often show because I am single and blokes would think I was on the pull. Thankfully, my time to relax and be myself will come, that's for sure.

At this point I can also hear (or anticipate) some of you asking why God allows us to suffer as we do: how come life, on the earth He supposedly created, isn't wonderful for all of us, all of the time?

He simply does not get involved, unless invited. He doesn't interfere. He set things in motion in the very beginning and now He watches, or rather His angels watch, as do His workers on earth (like me), to see how we react to and handle such disasters.

2 Chronicles 16:9: 'For the eyes of the Lord run to and fro throughout the whole earth, to show Himself strong in the behalf of them whose heart is perfect (= friendly) toward Him.' When He sees a friendly heart He occasionally, when absolutely necessary, intervenes or steps in to help. The people in question might not even be aware that it is Him.

God's intention, from the beginning, was that life on earth should be perfect and full of peace and love and joy and pleasure, but Satan, who was the highest ranking son of God (except for The number one Son) in heaven (very powerful and very charismatic and beautiful), decided that the power he had wasn't enough. He wanted the same authority and favour that God had given to His loved, firstborn Son (who eventually came to earth as Jesus). Consequently (and stupidly) Satan rebelled and challenged God and he and many other angels and sons of God who followed him, set about making their own plan. Please understand that angels are not silly plump cherubs with wings, these are beings who can take on human form and they have immense power and ability and are able to move around in the different dimensions. Basically angels are the heavenly equivalent of servants. One of the first things the ones who rebelled did was have sex with women on earth and produce giants. It tells us in Genesis that these sons of God saw earthly women and thought they would like some of that.

If anyone thinks that Hollywood invented time travel and fantastical beings and unearthly abilities and powers, they can think again. God Himself is far greater in power than anything or anyone in this world and there are indeed many spiritual and physical dimensions which we humans are not commonly or lightly permitted to see or experience. Anyway, Satan (and his followers) decided that they would prove that they were better than God and set about attempting to discredit God and destroy what He had made. They attempted to show that Satan is more powerful by persuading people that they don't need God.

God is three separate beings: in the simplest of terms they consist of our heavenly Father, who decided and planned what He wanted in creation (and in the heavenly dimensions also, of course); His firstborn Son, who is our guide and the Word or Voice of God to mankind and who declares His Father's will; and the Holy Spirit, who is the one who has the power to make things happen that God requires or commands. The Holy Spirit is also our helper and comforter and He sows the good seed of God in us. So when Satan rebelled, God basically said, 'Go ahead and ultimately all will see who is God, who is the most powerful etc'. There is no record of God having said this, but He said a similar thing when Satan singled out a guy called Job for a particularly nasty trial or beating (see the opening chapters of The Book of Job in the Old Testament).

Satan is not a horned creature, frolicking in a hell full of indulgent sensual pleasure; he is the master of disguise, the best impersonator and con artist; he is also bitter and vicious and cruel in extreme and he can also appear to be sweet as sugar, encouraging people to believe in all kinds of 'harmless' airy fairy magical and mystical nonsense as an alternative to the true way of God. He knows that his time in power is coming to an end and he is a desperate 'man'. He is also a sower of lies; he is the father of lies, *the* liar from the beginning. He is not interested in getting followers from this world, we mean nothing to him, all he is interested in is destroying God's plan and all of His that is good. A classic example of the lies he spreads is the well-used suggestion that this is the only life we have, so we might as well make the most of it!

He also sows discord, causing families and friends to fall out - the extreme example of this is wars between countries. He is the founder of many other religions and a manipulator of the truth (they have a ring of truth but often these religions involve humiliation for women and have stringent rules, which degrade and destroy or restrict their followers). He will stop at nothing to prevent anyone from believing in the true God, so that they suffer the agonies of Hell forever with him, simply because we are made by God. He wants to take as many as he can down with Him and He will stop at nothing to do so. And he is the master of distraction techniques. Do not be fooled by him. It is time to recognise his voice also.

Clearly my earthly life story is not unique (though I do have a reasonably clear understanding of the basics of the truth). Many prophets and righteous men and women throughout the ages have endured much greater suffering and torment to reveal the truth to mankind. The most prominent were God's own beloved Son Jesus Christ, The Prophet and the Messiah, who came initially for the Jews, who rejected Him as their Messiah because He didn't say what they wanted to hear and He was not attractive at all when He came as a man and was not what they expected - see Isaiah 53 which describes His earthly appearance and rejection. The Lord himself suffered ridiculous rejection, he was belittled and bullied, taken the piss out of and more; not only during his three year ministry in the public eye but throughout his short life. He was in His early thirties when He began His three year' ministry in the public eye and people thought he was in his fifties; he was worn out in the flesh.

Some of the prophets of old suffered terrible abuse, often publicly, in defence of the truth. As part of this process of writing to you I am compelled to reveal the torment that I, and others, in this present day have also endured as a consequence of being held captive against our will, after being deceived by a man whom we trusted. We are still suffering the backlash of this, to varying degrees. Many of our contemporaries have quit or fallen by the wayside, given up on the truth, listened to the lies of the enemy because the going has been tough, but the Lord understands; His grace is not exhausted for all of them yet.

Do not assume that if you choose to tune in to the Lord and believe Him that your life is going to be just as tough and miserable; we (I and my friends) have a particular calling and work to complete. Plus your life might already be tough so at least if you follow Him and your life continues to be shit, it will count for something. But He has assured me that relief is on its way. It won't be entirely bloody miserable... and anyway, 'He is coming', and I, for one, believe this is true; I believe His word emphatically.

* * * * *

This is THE true story of the triumph of good over evil: this is my witness to 'The Way, the Truth and the Life' from John 14:6: 'Jesus said unto him, 'I am The way, and The truth, and The life: no man cometh unto the Father but by Me'. Knowing the Father is a distinct privilege, but we cannot get close to the Father without first acknowledging the Son, Christ Jesus. This is my own personal account of my experience and my witness to the glory of the truth and it is through Him that we can know the truth about God, the Father of Life itself. (NB The early followers of the Lord/the Truth were called Followers of the Way; it was not until much later that they were called Christians. The Father is not excluding other faiths here; we all worship God, as Paul said, but the only way to be allowed into the presence of the Father Himself is to believe in Jesus Christ.)

At the time of writing I do not have the answer to how the Father came to be (for now I can accept that He just *is*), but I believe that one day He will explain this to me because I will ask the question, and He has promised to reveal all things and make all things clear.

My grandson asked me recently what God made everything out of when He made the earth. I will share the answer with you, in case you are also wondering. His power is like magic and is so great that He really can just say the word and what He needs appears. He formed the first man, Adam, out of clay and the holy Spirit breathed life into him. The creation of the worlds and the universe and mankind etc was, in our scope of understanding and experience, the first great miracle by God. But, of course, He made other things, other worlds, before He decided to make our Universes. This is not His first creation, nor His last.

These are the Last Hours of the Last days or the End days for this world and this is a message for all denominations and religions and believers in God. Originally the opportunity to know God (Jehovah) was the exclusive territory or privilege of the Jewish people, the Children of Israel, and then, after the Lord (Jesus) rose from the dead, this privilege was opened up to the rest of the world, on condition that they believe that the Lord Jesus Christ is the Son of God and the only way to know God was by faith in Him but, in these Last days the Lord has shown me that, in His grace and love for mankind, He is acknowledging the moral conviction and innate, inbuilt knowledge of good and evil that exists in people.

Many have rejected the teachings of the recognised Christian Church, as it is today, in its fragmented and divided forms. Others have turned to other faiths in search of the truth and inner peace and are attempting to make sense of the desire they have within themselves to believe that this crazy, messed-up world is not the end and that *Someone* is in charge and knows what is going on. In fact this world is only the beginning - the beginning of something much more wonderful and joyful and blessed (happy). The true way and message to mankind that the Lord died for has largely been lost, corrupted and contaminated, and this has caused many people to reject Him, when it is the leaders and many of the teachers of faith who are to blame (because some have believed the lies of the father of lies or not tried hard enough to do their job and find the whole truth, for whatever reasons).

In these last days God is showing that He has heard the genuine souls/people and is calling you to have confidence in Him. He is compassionate and loving and kind and patient and gracious and fun and irreverent (to those people who think they are holier and better than all us 'sinners' in this world). He is generous in His love for His creation, which includes us, His created children, and He knows that we are far from perfect. He knows what we are, in fact He made us this way. Real love for God is not about 'good works' designed to impress Him or convince Him or others that we are good. He sees the hidden goodness within us; He sees only the heart. He is not impressed by any of the accomplishments of man. He made everything that is of any value to us and, more significantly, to Himself, and He gave us intelligence. Nevertheless, everything is ours to enjoy, whether it is God given or manmade; *enjoy* being the operative word. He would not recommend or condone our continuing with anything once it has ceased to be a pleasure but He understands that some things, like alcohol and drugs, are addictive and controlling and it takes strong moral fibre to quit and, most importantly, a reason to quit or resist. Sometimes this is all we have to make life bearable.

Yet all these things become a dead end, and are a lie and a trap. If you are one of those people, be assured He has seen you and He is giving you a reason to take control, and for some of us this includes a reason to live, if you can hear Him now.

There is no denying that I too am battle weary (fucking punch drunk is wot I is), but I must assure you again that this is not primarily about my suffering or the Lord's suffering, (He climbed down off the cross the moment He died, but the 'Church' insists on leaving Him up there! HE DIED AND ROSE AGAIN, PEOPLE! And He is not a baby any more. Also the cross was the weapon that was used in a misguided attempt to silence and destroy Him!

I have been made to feel like a fraud by those who would silence me, as my life overall and outwardly is hardly a glowing advert for the life I am attempting to recommend, and also because the Lord has not immediately responded to some of my requests and fulfilled what He has promised me. The disciples had the same problem; there were those watching them who sneered, 'Where is the promise of His coming ...then?' with the insinuation that the disciples got it wrong. We will see who is right. I believe Him.

I understand why some others would condemn me at times and tell me I am wrong or misguided. I cannot deny either that on several occasions in recent weeks I have been tempted to jack it all in because of the extreme pressure from the Opposition (as we have come to call the enemy). He is as real as God is real and he is *the* opposer (proper poser!) and enemy of all that is good. He would attempt to persuade us that Hell is the better place to go... yeah, right! Ha! The Opposition does not want me to write this book and he has done his level best to discredit me and undermine my confidence; to literally break me. The Jewish prophet Jeremiah (chapter 20 v9) understood my present mood regarding my relationship with the Lord perfectly: 'Then (Jeremiah) said, 'I will not make mention of Him, nor speak any more in His name. But His word was in my heart as a burning fire shut up in my bones, and I was weary with forbearing (keeping it in, holding it back; it is a constant bloody battle), and I could not stay (= hold back)' and, like Jeremiah, I cannot not resist His pull. The Lord keeps drawing me back, propping me up; feeding that constant fire burning in my heart, which is much more powerful and wonderful than anything that the opposition or others can throw at me in an attempt, not only to stop me from declaring the truth but to literally destroy me; I have been pressured to contemplate ending it all several times, I even decided how I would do it if it came to it and wrote the letter for my son. I tried once before but now I know why it did not work and know how I would do it successfully; the enemy has made sure of that, so I cannot, must not, give him the satisfaction. That is his 'job'; his aim or mission, obsession in life is to prevent any of us from believing in God and to discredit us and Him (God, Jesus, Lord, Jehovah, Allah, whatever name you know Him by at this time) and he tries one way or another to destroy anyone who poses a serious threat to his plan. He knows he cannot stop me believing so he has to try to get me to top myself, to literally end my life, prevent me from being here.

Idols made from wood and other materials are an abomination. These are man-made gods and have nothing to do with the only supreme God, about whom I am speaking here. These idols are promoted by the Hindu and Catholic religions and others. These mystical idols and the lives of the people who are in bondage to them seem very attractive, but do not be deceived; it is all a colourful sham. The Jews and the Christians and the Muslims in particular, all originate from the same 'family' and worship the same God and Father of all. The divisions between us are a clear example of the work of the Enemy. It is incredibly sad.

I believe that God has time for untouched, remote tribes who have the most simplistic attitude to God, whom they see in nature and the forest world, which He created to provide for their everyday needs, around them. Their lives are probably the nearest to the way it was in the beginning for Adam and the woman. This is a different matter. Perhaps they will learn of the Lord Jesus Christ before He returns, or maybe they will meet Him for the first time, in the air. This is not my concern.

The final part of this second chapter includes an extract from the opening chapter of the gospel or teachings of John the Apostle, who was one of the Lord's disciples (an ordinary fisherman and a greatly loved disciple), called to walk and work with the Lord Jesus Christ, God's Son. (Apostle simply means 'one who has been sent'.) The Lord was, and is, 'that Prophet or The Prophet' who chose of His own free will to do His Father's will on earth. I must explain that His earthly name Jesus is precious because it represents His earthly calling and suffering, which enabled Him to experience and understand and empathise with the human struggle: He had to learn who He was and find His work on earth, in exactly the same way that we/I have. He walked by faith, to bring us all to a place where we can accept that we can indeed talk directly to God and show that He does want to communicate with us, His children. I was taught (and believed, like many other people) that we are adopted children of God, by the leader of the cult, who did not 'rightly divide or understand, the word of truth', but the Bible/ the Word actually says something very different, through the teachings of Paul the apostle. I can explain (for those of you who do not know of him) that Paul was a strict and zealous Jew and a Roman, who initially consented to the murder of Christians (see the book of Acts chapter 8 etc for more details, if you wish) before the Lord called him and changed his mind (I believe Catholics call this 'Paul's conversion', like he had an upgrade, which I suppose he did. See Acts 9). He was not a nice bloke at that time and had to bear the burden of knowing what he had done, in his religious zeal, for the rest of his life.

But, getting back to adoption – Paul actually wrote (see Galatians 4:4), 'But when the fullness of the time was come (or when the end of the previous era in God's plan had been accomplished or fulfilled), God sent forth His Son (Jesus Christ), made of a woman (He had to experience life as we know it and had to learn who He was, just like us), made under the Law, to redeem (save and free) them that were under the Law.' He came to the Jews first because they were God's original chosen people and had to live by strict rules, which God had imposed to keep them safe basically, until it was time for His Son to come and show them a more relaxed way. I realise that I have already mentioned this fact and others several times, this is His way, but you will notice that I have also added to your understanding with each reference or each time I mention these things. The Lord Jesus was born a Jew and was subject to the regulations of the Law, otherwise none of the Jews would have accepted Him. They were, and are, a very arrogant nation because they know that God, Jehovah, said they were special, but what they don't appreciate is that they were simply a sign and God put the right spirit or heart into Abraham, their earthly father or patriarch. Abram, or Abraham as he became, wanted to please God: he had respect for God and believed in Him. The Jews/Israelites as a nation, those who still live under the Law (of Moses; the Ten commandments etc) remain arrogant, not realising that we are *all* now special and blessed and that they are no different to us, other than they missed His first coming, so they have nothing to brag about!

This next part of the quotation is where ministers can go wrong. Paul continues '*that we might receive the adoption of sons.*' I can explain that when we adopt something we make it our own and in a sense we are adopted by the Lord because we have a relationship with Him, but we need to also grasp that we are connected to Him from the womb. He made a way for us to be formed in the womb and the Spirit is put in us from God, in the womb, to be not only His friends but also His sons and daughters. So, He is our real Father. His Spirit is put in those of us who can hear His voice, we have come from Him. How He did this, exactly how He made anything, will remain a mystery for now; I assume it is beyond us to grasp this, but perhaps not impossible; it's a bit like magic, as I already explained. I personally believe He did it in much the same way that some of us can make things, if we have the right components and materials. But then we might ask, 'Where did He get these parts from?' Let's face it, He's God; He can do anything and we could send ourselves mad (which is what happens to crazy professors, who profess to know everything). We too would go crazy if we cannot simply just accept that *He is* (God)... and *He can* (do whatever He wants).

I do recall someone explaining to me once upon another lifetime that everything is made from light, but physics isn't my strong point, so I cannot provide details. More important is the realisation that He is our real Father. Wow! No stigma to that. No second best. No shame in that, eh? We can call Him Father if we can accept that the Spirit of the Father and His first created Son is in us, in our hearts, within or inside us from the womb (ie the Holy or heavenly Spirit). The Holy Spirit is everywhere.

Ministers have led us to believe that true spirituality, which is often portrayed on the one hand as a lovey-dovey soppy, bloody, self-righteous, holy act and on the other something that individuals and groups are prepared to murder others and become martyrs for in support of their zeal for God. There is a middle ground (the fighting is over - he is here. True spirituality is attainable for us ordinary mortals, although it is made to appear out of reach, mystical and complicated and the deep truths are only for a select few, but it is actually very simple and available for all! It is simply about being real and honest with Him and listening or seeing or feeling Him in your heart. Hopefully this book will help you to understand this. You can have whatever you can grab, however much you want. It's all good and we will be happy in eternity, if we accept His invitation.

Getting back to John, however, his initial advice, written centuries ago, shows how powerful and descriptive and enduring the Word of God (the Bible) is and how His Word continues to be relevant and can still speak to us today, in this fragmented and troubled society. For many years the Bible, His written word, was the only way God talked to and communicated with me (and with my friends and contemporaries).

Stick with me Reader - I apologise for not knowing or having the space to use your names individually, and anyway I am trusting that there is more of you reading this than Babsi and Jordi and the Daves and Johns and Rab and Pete and Chris and Claire and Sally and Fee and Mandy and all the Steves (to name but a few that I have known). Please indulge me for one moment here. The word of God for me is a treasure trove of hope and love and assurance and understanding about a very real Lord and God and friend and Father, in this often harsh and tedious world, and there is nothing on this earth that can set me on fire quite like it. He does however speak to me in many other ways, as you will see in the following chapters, if or when I work from my journals and notes. There might not be time as I have to get the basics across before I can move on with my life, my walk.

This is the beginning of our faith/life with God, the beginning of our understanding of Him; this is a message that runs consistently throughout the word and especially the New Testament (= new promise):

John 1:1-13: 'In the beginning was the Word, and the Word was with God, and the Word was God (God is three separate beings, as I explained, but they have one purpose, They are in total agreement). The same Word (He is more commonly known as Lord or Jesus) was in the beginning (before the world was made). He was (part of) God'.

The Word is another of the Lord's names. He was the first being that God, the Father of all, created or made and He speaks on behalf of God, our Father.

'All things were made by Him; and without Him was not anything made that was made. In Him was life (the life or essence of God); and that life was, and is, the light of men. And the light shined in darkness and the darkness comprehended it not'. The darkness comprehended it not; what does this mean, you could be asking? I certainly was, and I am going to take another look at it now. Please take a look at it yourself, if you want, and ask for understanding, and you may get more or something different. It is not set in stone as the Jewish Law was.

John was speaking on the one hand about the dark side of the character of men and women. The truth is not easy to accept, partly because of the way it is presented but also because people prefer not to know because they fear it (fear of the unknown again! And it might mean they have to do something, make a commitment, God forbid!). For some insane reason many people prefer to believe in a temporary existence on this earth or a load of 'old wives' tales' and nonsense. How many times have we all heard the old saying, (which I have already quoted), 'You only have one life so you have to make the most of it'. My thought is consistent because of my own life experience but your answer might differ, 'If this is really it, then some of us have definitely drawn the short straw'. If reincarnation is true I shall be even more disappointed when I make it to nothing.

It is narrow-minded to imagine that God only created us and everything else that He made on this earth just to end it here or to punish us for all eternity. This life is the place where we decide who we are going to believe, and I can guarantee that Heaven will far exceed our wildest imaginings of what the ideal life would entail, including the best party, but I do look forward to taking my seat at His table and the after party.

The other aspect of this truth 'the darkness comprehended it not' is that light and dark are two very separate entities. When we enter an utterly dark room and switch on a light, for example, the darkness is still there but the light invades the darkness, it enables us to see other things in the room because it is stronger, more powerful, even though we cannot actually see light itself; the light overpowers, is stronger than, the darkness.

There are two meanings for the word 'comprehended'; firstly light is always more dominant and more powerful than darkness, whether it is spiritual darkness and light or physical darkness and light. The darkness/the enemy can never overcome or be stronger than The light, ie God. It is beyond the scope or experience or capacity of darkness to understand the light and it can never drown the light out because of how it is constructed or made. Therefore the Light, as in His guiding and cleansing spiritual light, can never be extinguished or overcome by the darkness or wickedness of the Wicked one (the enemy/the Devil). Neither can he comprehend or understand the light any longer; he cannot grasp it and has forgotten how powerful it is. He believes that he is still here is of any consequence to God. But he is underneath God and is no longer visible because God's light overpowers or over-rides him and shines and it will keep shining for all eternity. The world without God would be a very dark place... *is* a very dark place, with no light to show the way out. Understanding is light, and this is why I trust that you can understand these explanations.

I recently learned that the only instance when actual darkness is stronger than light is in a black hole, created when a massive star dies. This is a small example of what will happen when the sun eventually dies. The death of the sun, combined with other catastrophic events, will cause everything to be sucked in to the black hole it will create and the universe in which we live, and those beyond, will all fold in on itself. This is what is prophesied in the Bible. I do not have the full knowledge of all the details at this time or the time or inclination to find out but the pertinent points here are that this world and all the stars and every aspect of this creation, apart from His people, the ones whom He rescues, will eventually end and that the Father also created or introduced darkness for His purposes, this being one example.

However, as I said, I am easily distracted. There is so much to tell and so little time, but I must also continue to explain that the Lord did come to earth as a man. He had the same feelings and weaknesses as us and He had to believe in the same way we do. He had to learn very quickly because Satan knew who He was from the moment Jesus was born and he tried his best to extinguish His light (the light in terms of the understanding He brought) through King Herod, who killed all the newborn babies in the surrounding area within days of the Lord's birth, because he was provoked to believe that Jesus would take over his position as king. If the Lord (Jesus) had given up and given in to the pressure that He would have been under more or less constantly to believe the doubts and the lies, then Satan would have won. He would have extinguished the light of the world, taken away all hope and removed everyone's opportunity to ever learn about and understand the truth about God and the Way to a heavenly eternity. This had to be a very real possibility and shows the calibre and guts of the Lord as a man, Jesus (there is no wonder they thought he was in His fifties when He was only in His early thirties). He deserves our praise and thanks because He certainly paid the price, not only on the cross but throughout His short life. He knows and understands our suffering and He has made a way out. Think on this and Praise Him indeed!

We all have our burdens and crosses to bear or carry and we get new ones as the old ones fade, but He has no desire to add to that burden of life. He only wishes to make it lighter and remove the fears and other things that make life hard to bear for some of us. If your life is OK then thank Him for that, be thankful; simply acknowledge Him. He has no desire to interfere in your life. He loves us. God is love; it's as simple as that.

CHAPTER 4

I am winging it with this fourth chapter: I do not yet have much of a clue about what I will be saying. I do know that at some stage I must confine myself to clarifying or making clear the Message, which is not a new message in itself. It is the message which the Lord brought and which could have been fulfilled in His day, if the Jews, as a nation, had recognised that Jesus was their Messiah. His disciples and others taught this same message and others have continued to do so throughout the centuries. Now, in these End days, the message is being broadcasted once more for all to hear, in a way that all should relate to. I trust that my work here will be rewarded and it will be published and read and discussed by many. My conviction that this is His will/His work is strong because He has strengthened me for this, because otherwise I would talk myself out of it in a heartbeat. I am increasingly knackered but, although I feel even more worn out, today I feel blessed. I have been typing on and off all day and I am determined to type up the notes I was given earlier this morning because the stuff is mounting up but I do feel blessed and happy because I can see finally that I am making progress and that He is definitely leading me in this. It is His will. I am not wrong in any shape or form, whatever anyone else might think. I feel exhausted but relieved.

I will never in a million years be able to type up what there is to know and say (I don't know it all by any stretch of the imagination anyway). You will have to ask Him to show you the rest of it for yourself, if you want more, when I have finished. We need an eternity!

I don't know all of it, but He speaks to me daily and has done so for many years on and off. I have no desire to ask Him to stop giving me understanding because I am a greedy cow and this is a never-ending treasure trove. I do get a bit overwhelmed with it all sometimes, but He is pushing and encouraging me to get on with it; it blows my mind. He knows I am a woman and He also knew this when He chose me for this job. He knows I like to talk (fortunately especially about Him) and I have trouble keeping to the point, staying focused. I am easily excited, especially about this stuff. I am in my element. I can't type very fast and the laptop and the net are alien to me, but they are minor details after what I have been through to get here. He will help me to work it out.

Things are definitely looking up! Today is a good day! Phew, it has been too long a road.

⋆ ⋆ ⋆ ⋆ ⋆

It has been difficult for me to know how to go about this, writing to you, knowing exactly what to say (though I am doing it!); revealing not only things about Him but laying my life out for all to see. I forget that it is necessary for me to show you all these things because I am as you are, as He was, and He is a part of me and my own life experience is evidence of Him. It is all wrapped up together, so that you know that my faith has endured. He must be with me; it must be true.

Until quite recently the Lord and the Father have communicated with me or spoken directly to me, and my close friends, through the Bible, in the way that I have explained. This was the only way I heard His voice. However, since we left the cult my world has opened up. I have had vivid memories of past lives; He has spoken to me via signs on the side of lorries and billboards and through dreams, and He has given me messages through lyrics and shapes in the clouds. He has used nature and the stars. It is as if He is bombarding me because He understands what a challenge this is. It has been quite incredible.

Last year I travelled around Europe with a close friend, sleeping in a tent, following the signs. It was our way of breaking free of the physical ties of our old life; it was a working holiday; quite traumatic at times and hard work, but incredibly liberating and a confidence builder for me. I had to trust Him totally because only a few months previously I had still been in the grip of ME.

One morning recently I was sitting in the café at the Welcome Break services (a welcome place of escape and contemplation for me at the moment) asking Him for help with the book, telling the Lord that I was not even convinced that I was doing the right thing because I felt as if I was completely out of my depth, when I caught a line of the lyrics of the song that was playing: 'you have to find a way to say what you want to say'.

The following is extracted directly from the notes I have

written today in my notebook, after watching the people around me come and go, at Welcome Break funnily enough!

'People are the same wherever we go in the world (I just noticed I almost quoted the words from the Beatles track, as I was reading it back, and its true what they said). People are replicated over and over. In my role as a Watcher I notice people, individuals and couples, and while they might not look exactly the same, essentially they are the same, either in looks or characteristics. Some people attempt to stand out and be individual by dressing differently or behaving differently, but there are only so many human permutations. It is our soul that is individual and unique.

Some people do achieve individuality to some extent, but then as they get older they start to notice that they are morphing into their mum or dad and start behaving or sounding like them. This is hard to resist. If you have noticed this happening then I'm guessing you don't have a lot else to worry about, so be grateful. Those who don't know who their birth parents are can be assured that they will have some of the mannerisms of their earthly mother or father, because quite clearly some of it is programmed into our genes, if complete strangers also have the same characteristics. I seem to be digressing, but there is a point to this, so bear with me.

We make too much of our human heritage, our roots, and that is because most of us have a need, a basic desire, to belong. Knowing that we have come from Him and that one day we will return to Him is much more profound and meaningful. I suppose that most people want to know because they want to believe that they have something good and worthwhile or notable inside them. Surely not many would like to think that they are a complete tosser from a line of tossers? Others say they don't give a crap, but I find that one hard to believe.

At this point I have to tell you that I am no longer strongly suicidal and I know this because I left a note this morning for my housemates which said, 'I have gone for a long walk off a short pier'. This is noteworthy because although I could make jokes about myself when I was constantly suicidal, as my opinion of my own self-worth was so low, I would never have used this one because this is what my Dad would say when I was a kid (the same as saying 'go and play with the traffic') and I love my earthly dad; he would never have intentionally hurt me. This might seem like a small thing but to me, and to God, it is quite significant.

The purpose in me telling you this about ('finally' I hear you sigh), is that all that matters to the Lord (I know I keep saying this and I will probably say it again) is that we *believe* that He has seen us and that we do our best and keep listening to that still small voice within us, the voice we know as conscience. It doesn't matter if you don't come from a good family background, it means nothing to Him except that He will reward parents who are kind to their children and love them, even though it is not always easy (they are only on loan to us); He passionately *detests* child abuse, all children are innocent and precious. All of us have some awareness of good and evil remaining in us from the womb and some parents do their best to teach their children what is basically good and what isn't, but ultimately we all make our own choices in life. Good is written in our hearts.

Hope is not lost, even if life has dealt you a crap hand and you feel that you are worthless. I was deceived by that pile-of-crap cult leader into treating my kids harshly, and I am only now able to believe it was not my fault and forgive myself.

Occasionally we have to be firm with our children to give them safe boundaries to live within. Some believe that the bible teaches us that we should use the rod or the stick to keep our children in place, but this is emphatically *not* what it says. It is easy to see how we could come to this conclusion, but we are also told to 'rightly divide the word of truth'. We have to look at the meanings of the original Hebrew or Greek words; some things have been badly translated. For example (Proverbs 13:24) 'He that spares the rod (stick) hates his son: but he that loves him chastens him often'. *Spare* in Hebrew means to darken, so if we darken the stick, or use it against our kids as a punishment then we hate them. But, if we love them we guide them and instruct and warn and teach them often; and do it with love, not fear. I need to explain this because too many children still suffer this abuse. I wish I had not trusted the guy in charge because I was guilty of smacking my children and more being too strict with them because he didn't teach the truth; he convinced us that our children would go to hell if we didn't discipline them. It grieves me immensely now that I was so afraid and naive but I was living in fear and he was in a position of trust and I *was* vulnerable and naive. That pile of crap will be held accountable.

As I was thinking about this I wondered again what the prospect is for murderers, because it does say in the Bible that liars and abusers and child molesters and murderers and so forth have no place in the kingdom of heaven. I wonder if this still applies or does it depend on whether they are prepared to genuinely change their minds? Is it possible to stop being a full-blown liar (who never speaks the truth) or a murderer? What depths do people sink to that determines there is literally no more hope? What makes God turn His face away completely and the heavens to become like stone? Only God Himself would know if a murderer was genuinely repentant and sorry. He or she would have to serve the prison sentence, but eternally they might achieve grace if they find a conscience.

The problem with all these things is that they are like a drug and are addictive; unless someone or something else takes control it is very hard to stop. Though I am no angel I lie occasionally (and I think some bad stuff) like anyone else and the Lord knows it; in fact, His advice regarding being thoroughly honest (found in Psalms or Proverbs, 'be not over much something... honest'), is not to be too honest, otherwise people take advantage of you, among other things. And for murderers I guess it must depend on what causes them to cross that line (or liars and so forth for that matter). Once again it also depends on whether they still have a shred of genuine conscience towards God and decency and whether they can see that what they have done is not acceptable but, more significantly, that there is a way out.

The bloke who was in charge of our group cannot see or won't accept that he has done anything wrong. We are told that if we do not believe the truth then we *will* believe Satan's lies; there is no middle ground. To make it to heaven murderers and such like (and unbelievers) have to change their mind, their way of thinking before they die. I myself have had to do that (I have never murdered anyone; Paul the apostle consented to the murder of Christians before he saw the light and heard the Lord's voice).

We can be most sincerely very wrong, but don't panic because for most of us this simply means opening our minds to the truth, in order to put it right. Very often an apology to the Lord is all that is required, and to ask for forgiveness. Make no mistake, there are some who need to ask forgiveness. He will forgive most things and never mention them again.

Murderers and abusers must resolve to ask for His help to control that urge, because they could not do it by themselves; they must seek help from Him to really change and mean it. Simply being locked up in prison doesn't take away the desire to kill or abuse. The guilt must be too much to bear, if the desire to change is genuine, and only the Lord would be able to judge whether it is true repentance and provide the necessary help from a therapist and a touch from the Holy Spirit. The Jewish nation consented to the murder of the Son of God and yet they will be given another chance because they were deceived by the Pharisees (extremists) and others who were in charge. The individuals who were the ring leaders will suffer in Hell for all eternity that is certain.

Clearly all is not lost, even in some extreme cases. I thank the Lord that I am not called upon to kill as some are, in the armed forces for example, much less have the desire to murder someone in cold blood. I understand why some do though. I seriously feel I could have done so at one point; killed that man, that 'pile of dung' (pile of crap or shit is what the Lord called him, and He called him a cock/prick; God doesn't mince His words), that evil man who robbed me and my friends of the remainder of our innocence and all those years and took advantage of our trust.

I have to add that the mistake that 'do gooders' and some authorities make is they assume that there is that basic desire in everyone to change and do the right thing, or be right. Really wicked people run rings around these idiots and I myself was fooled by that thing (the pile of shit, POS), who appeared to be good; it is not easy to distinguish without His help. The Lord permitted me and my friends to be blinded by the pile of shit's lies for a long time (he blinded himself, the stupid f...ing idiot), in order to give him a chance or time to change his mind and ways.

I know it is in my power to destroy someone's life with words, and to me this is as destructive and wicked and insidious as actually murdering someone (these are some of the terrible thoughts that I was talking about). I have come into contact with people who are basically naïve, guileless and essentially harmless, who take the mickey out of me or make fun of me, and I could so easily destroy them with words if I was to retaliate fully, as I sometimes want to, because I have been feeling so vulnerable and defensive. But what would be the gain in that? Momentary satisfaction and then massive remorse and the Lord would never condone it because it would be deliberate on my part. A small amount of bitchiness is human nature.

My second husband was guileless as a young man (he would not have betrayed me like the POS minister. The Lord told me that my ex wouldn't betray me when we first met, but by the time we separated the Lord said he was cruel. (I was slightly older than him but I was still very naive in some ways.) Our life together was spoiled by the cult leader (POS), and hindered by the fact that I became ill and my husband wasn't honest and open enough about how he felt and what was going on. We all keep things back for one reason or another. I could not have prevented this decline, any more than I could have prevented my eldest son from killing himself. They made their own choices. It was never in my heart to intentionally hurt either of them. I know this now, but it has taken some time for me to get over the guilt I have felt. I have blamed myself, but I have come to see that I could not have altered things; I did what I could. I was a victim myself but, thank God, I am finally resolving things and working my way through it. I am bruised and battered, but I have lost none of my eternal reward and my conscience is clear. We all make our choices.

One of our main faults as human kind is that we are too ready or quick to judge others (and very easily persuaded to do so). We forget sometimes that we all have flaws and faults which annoy and hurt others, but it does not mean that we always have to change or lose our identities. Some people fool themselves into believing that they are good people but reveal their true nature in the things they say and do. The Lord is the only one who can make that final judgment. He is the only one without fault and He has seen everything. He sees hearts. In the end my second husband closed his heart to the truth, to the Lord, not only to me. I sincerely hope he has worked things through himself and found his peace. Sometimes He tells some of us that we can judge, but we have to treat this one with care and not get arrogant with it.

We are taught 'love never fails', but sometimes our love clearly fails, or has a limit. Love that is not reciprocated or is abused or taken for granted generally dies, unless He keeps it alive. Does His love fail; is there a limit to His love? I do know that He turns His face away from some people and lets them get on with it, to suffer the consequences, but it takes a long time for Him to do this. He is incredibly patient and long suffering. He knows what is in mankind, in the hearts of men and women. I believe He turns His back and gives up when people are determined to hold on to what they believe, when they have been shown there is need for change and also when people set out to prove they are better than others or decide that they do not need God. It is this defiance that determines there is only slender hope. I have to say 'slender' because people do sometimes cry to Him on their death bed and He snatches them from the fire. Continued defiance, even as someone is dying, is when all hope is finally lost. This is the mind and way of the Devil who tried, in his defiance against God, to destroy Jesus Christ and failed. The victory over death and the devil is won already, however. And it is because the Lord Jesus triumphed and the Devil failed that there is still so much hope and compassion, and there is very nearly always a way. There is always a way, if we are prepared to take His outstretched hand. I recognise that this might sound very schmaltzy and sickly because I am using over-used terminology, which for some might be difficult to swallow. On the other hand it might be the very familiarity of these phrases that is a comfort. It's a bloody minefield for me to find the correct expressions/words to suit everyone.

There are times when it feels as if God is not listening or has abandoned me and my life. What He expects from me is just too much and I myself have literally wanted to die and even turn away from Him in the frustration I have felt. Thankfully, I have learned over the years that at times like that the answer is always to draw nearer to Him. I thank God again that I can generally do this without thinking, because sometimes I cannot think I am so numbed by the psychological pain (I trust He will not let me go). The answer is basically to talk to Him; my first instinct is to praise God, which simply means I tell Him how amazing He is (which isn't easy when you feel He has deserted you), and then I seek His strength, His mercy (kindness), whatever it is that I need to help me to keep going. It was especially necessary when I was very ill and also when I have been suicidal, because I have felt so alone and life has not got any easier in recent months; it is getting harder to bear in some ways. Honestly, I don't know how much more I can take.

I realise that Satan is putting the pressure on and he would rejoice if he could stop me writing this, but equally importantly I know I would hurt the Father and badly let Him down if I topped myself; I have gone through too much and come too far. I have to trust even more that He will be faithful to His promise that there is blessing and happiness to come when I get to the other side of this particular time in my life. I am not the only one who has felt like chucking in the towel. Those of us who left the fellowship (a word I use lightly in this respect) we were in have all felt desperate at different times. Perhaps not to the point of wanting to die; I cannot be certain. I personally genuinely believed that my family and friends would be better off without me around, and I still do; this feeling has not gone away (at the time of typing) but I know I must finish this work and I refuse to believe that the Lord will let me, or them, down: He will vindicate my faith and trust in Him, and my actions in facing up to that revolting man. That basically is what keeps me going for now, and, of course, the promise that we will be going home very soon.

Jesus Himself knows what this feels like, even though He is The Son of God and knew that He was equal to His Father, when He was on Earth (Hebrews 5:7,8) 'Who in the days of His flesh, when He had offered up prayers and supplications with *strong* crying and tears unto Him that was able to save Him from death and was heard in that He feared' (it is a sacrifice/it costs to pray to God when you feel like this and the Father treasures these prayers like an expensive offering).

Paul was explaining that the Lord could see the hatred towards Him that was building up daily and He realised that they would be coming for Him very soon. He went into the garden in Gethsemane and prayed and He cried bitter tears that night. (The three disciples who were with Him, Peter, James and John, fell asleep because they could not bear to see Him like that – we are told they 'slept for sorrow'; it was just too heart wrenching for them to watch.) The Lord Jesus knew that He was soon going to die a dreadful, excruciating death on the cross. As far as was possible He was prepared for this, but no man in His right mind, even knowing that it was the perfect will of God, would rejoice at such a prospect. He wanted to die there and then, He wanted His Father to take Him. There is no doubt that He was terrified; He felt every bit as scared as we would do. These were 'the days of His flesh': He was a real flesh and blood man with all the emotions of a man with the capacity to feel pleasure and pain and He was shattered and thin/emaciated, worn out by this time. As He hung on the cross He could look down and see His bones sticking out. It is all too harrowing to think about. The cross is a weapon (please don't wear it round your neck!) It annoys me more than I can say that ministers encourage us to leave Him up there in our minds. He has risen from the dead people! He is now victorious and glorious! He had worked hard and had very little sleep and He must have felt as if He had nothing more to give as He earnestly prayed/talked to His Father in the garden, and yet He knew that the authorities were coming to get Him and He knew exactly what was coming.

He would have often gone into the Garden or into the hills and mountains around Jerusalem at night, when it was quiet, away from the crowds, to spend time with the Father, to give thanks and seek the strength to face another day (which is why He had little sleep and looked so rough) but He saw the signs and knew this next day would be different, the climax of His life on earth had arrived. Often these disciples, who were closest to Him, would have gone with Him (see Matthew 26 v36 etc for details of this particular night and day). He had spoken several times to all the disciples about what was going to happen to Him, yet for them it hadn't really sunk in. It wasn't until after He had risen/reappeared that they remembered His words and really understood. But the truth is He wanted to die there and then in the garden, to avoid the agony that was coming. He cried bitter tears because He felt that He did not have the strength to go on, but He finished His prayers every time by saying He still wanted to do His Father's will and go to the cross. He understood what was at stake and He believed and trusted that everything would be different when it was over; not only for Himself but for mankind. I have had a taste of His agony and I am not the only one I am sure. He did ask the disciples for help, to pray with Him, but this was just too much for them to handle and He did not blame them; He understood. This is all very real.

* * * * *

A bigger shock was yet to come when on the cross His Father did actually abandon Him (He died under the Law and according to that Earthbound Law He was cursed of God) but He had to continue to have faith that a new way was coming as a result of His sacrifice, even as He was dying completely and utterly alone, cut off from God. He had always, all His life, known His Father's presence with Him; He had never ever known what it feels like to be completely and utterly alone, cut off from His and our Father. He had to literally hang on and continue to believe (as He was suffering the agonies of death on that cross) that His faith was justified; that He had not made up or imagined the whole thing; He had to hold on to the knowledge that He had been given the ability to walk out of hell, that hell could not hold Him and then go back and speak to the women who had cared for Him and His disciples and then go up to His Father and take His own crown and sit on His throne to reign forever as King of kings.

The temptation to ask God to miraculously save Him must have been huge (and there were legions of angels just waiting for the word to intervene, they had not been told in advance what was actually happening); Satan would not have eased off at that crucial point, he would still have been whispering in his ear, telling Him to curse or blame God, and in addition, one of the blokes hanging beside Him appealed to Him to ask God to save the three of them and the soldiers mocked Him and some people scornfully said that 'He saved others so let's see if He can save Himself'.

We can only deduce or take a stab at knowing exactly what He was thinking by knowing or imagining how we would feel in similar, less extreme, circumstances. It was desperate and yet He cried out, 'forgive them Father for they know not what they do'. They hadn't a fucking clue what was going on! He is amazing. What a man. He is just the best! There is no other man quite like Him. Even as He was suffering as an innocent man He assured the guy beside Him, who *had* committed a crime, that night they would both be in paradise (which tells me that He went home to see His Father before He went to hell and then after that He returned to assure His followers that He was okay). The rest is history, as someone said. He went down to hell triumphant and rose again. No more tears for Him; no more pain and doubt or fear or uncertainty: He has beaten death itself, our greatest fear, the greatest unknown because He has prepared the way. There is now a way back, or rather forward, for us. We just have to follow in His footsteps, across the final field of snow.

You could be asking, 'What on earth is she on about now?' Give me a chance to explain, as I generally do.

Today I myself am racked by self-doubt again. I read through what I have written already and wonder who the hell is going to read beyond the first few lines. I must remember not to write my own recommendations. That's not the word I am looking for but excuse me, my brain is mashed. I am doing reasonably well on the no swear words thing, but without them I feel it is missing some of my pain and passion. I dislike people with no passion. They are like cold greasy dish water. Boring and revolting! That's just my opinion, by the way, I dunno what the Lord thinks. Not a good start today, eh? You get my mood?

OK... deep breath... keep going... focus!

My close friends and I believe in the baptism of the Holy Spirit (as do others, of course; speaking in tongues is the proof that His spirit lives in us). We can speak and pray and sing in tongues and we can prophesy and interpret in the Spirit, ie the Holy Spirit speaks through us, directly answers our prayers, which we speak in other tongues/languages (see 1 Corinthians 12 and Acts 2 for details). I use the snow picture as a way of describing this because this is how the Holy Spirit Himself described it (and I trust you know what a field of snow looks like, even if it is only from a photo). I too wondered why He used this way of describing it.

A field of fresh snow looks harmless and clean and inviting and white, but lurking beneath could be all kinds of danger. And this world can often look a lot like that, therefore it makes sense, and it is far safer, to follow the imprints He has made. Also, footprints in fresh snow are clear to see. I understand that until now many of us have been wading through mud in lead-filled boots (it was exactly the same for Jesus, as you have heard) but I am convinced that He has now provided the cushion of compacted snow on a flat field for this final leg home, for those of us who are listening to this, right now.

Speaking of the 'last leg', you might also be interested to know that the competitors in the longer races in the original Olympic Games were awarded extra points if they helped others who were in difficulty along the way. It was only when they reached the final 100 metres or yards or so (or whatever the Greek measurements were in those days) that they were expected to make a dash for the finishing post. We are now on this final dash for the finish, so basically it is 'every man for himself'. I realise some will struggle with this, but if we dither now and keep looking around at what others are doing, we might veer off the path and fall into a ditch and someone else will muscle in and take our heavenly crown. It's up to you. Or we can hold hands; sounds soppy I know but I can't let go (like the twat that I am, but I am glad we can all hold His hand). I am happy to get to the back (again I must be crazy; strengthened is a better word) and follow you in. You can think it's soppy or pathetic if you like, and if you do then you deserve to be on your own. This might sound like a load of bollocks but this is serious stuff and I'm going to believe it because I am sick of trudging through the crap! If others want to stay and wallow in it, that is their choice. This shitty world is going down and it is not going to improve. This world is spiralling into chaos, make no mistake.

The cynical among you will say, as they did in His day and many times since then no doubt, that we have been in recession before, there have been many disasters and others who seem like nutters (they are in fact convicted by the truth) have warned, 'the End is nigh'. Well, the very end of this world is not going to happen just yet (I will explain a little more about what's in store for those who are still here when He has been to collect those of us who believe in a later chapter) but I can say with confidence, it is going to be tougher than tough for those who are still here for the long haul. There will be *nothing* to celebrate and some people will be desperately crying out to Him to do something (especially the Jews) and others will be cursing Him. It will be extremely hard and bleak. Mark my words! Mark His words! It is all foretold.

I am not pleading with you to believe these facts about the Lord and our Father and His will and ways and the things that are coming. If you can hear His call, you have nothing to fear; you *will* hear (the trumpet on the day He appears; the ears of the deaf will be opened and the scales will fall from the eyes of the blind) and you will understand (to whatever degree); it is a lot to take in and accept but I trust the Holy Spirit will do His work, His part, and strengthen your faith, your God-given ability to hear Him. This is not a begging letter; it is evidence of the great love that God has for His creation and His created children and He would prefer it if none were lost. I have been one of those who are up front in the race and now, I have just realised, I *am* coming up the rear (pardon the expression!)... kind of like a sheep dog. This is the helping push, the safety light that He is providing; I strongly advise that you take it. I *am* being strengthened myself, despite how it sounds, and enabled to give you the facts and explain the truth and it is up to you to choose based on what you have been shown. And there is more to come. I will show you the victory, and the prize and the good things of God. All that you need to do is hear and accept His invitation: as He said to me all those years ago, simply 'open your heart and let Him in'; He will do the rest. He has promised. He has promised...

I took a break after this and now there is a battle raging inside my head because I am being provoked by well-meaning friends and family. This is like an open therapy session, except I can guarantee I won't be saying exactly what I would say in session with my therapist/counsellor and in my times talking to the Lord. He knows I have to unburden, otherwise I would really blow my stack. It is 'one of those days'. I feel very lonely, alone. I am sure some around me think I am a misguided waster, doing this. No worries, I'll get over it.

It feels like an inappropriate moment to say this, but we can now have peace with God. I have peace with God but not necessarily with everyone else, or with myself. I am still shackled to this world and its fearful and sceptical limitations.

Time for a break: I am here to help you not to vent my own spleen. I will be back tomorrow; refreshed and ready to encourage... I trust! (Monday 6th August 12)

This morning my mind is once again filled with the same dark thoughts and I wonder if I will ever get out of this pit. However, when I stepped outside I noticed a tiny frog thrashing around in the metal dog bowl. He has apparently been there for a couple of days and I had not realised previously (I am slow on the uptake, poor little bugger) that he was unable to get out because the sides are too smooth. I placed a long leaf in there for him to climb on to but he was exhausted and panicking so I lifted him out and he hopped into the undergrowth. Simply because he is a frog, designed to live in water, does not mean that he cannot drown. If I had left him there with the leaves, he would have rested and eventually climbed out by himself, but it was safer for him to rest protected by the undergrowth. This is a clear example of how the Lord speaks to me and answers my prayers and my /our cries for help.

So how does this help you and me in our present circumstances? The pit we are thrashing around in seems to have smooth sides and its pretty dark down here in the slimy, shitty water, but be assured the Lord has thrown a rope down into this pit. Take a deep breath and rest a while and then hold on to that rope and He will pull you out. The rope is His promises. For you this might simply be the messages contained in this book. He has answered your cries for help.

Take the rope! Hold on to these promises, as they are absolutely true. God has seen you; He has heard you, now it is your turn to hear and trust Him.

And I too must trust His promises to me. I must believe that every word is true and that everything They have promised will be fulfilled in our Father's time, in His way. Despite what others might say I must continue to believe His promises to me personally. I must not let go. I am wearing myself out, thrashing about listening to other voices, doubting and blaming Him. I know that He is true and faithful. I know His voice and I must stand firm and He will vindicate my faith. Take another deep breath woman... push it out! Onwards and upwards!

I have just seen my counsellor today, and she confirmed that it is OK and understandable for me to feel anger. It is a very alien emotion to me and it is rooted in the abuse I have lived through and my recent rejection. In the course of my sessions with her I will be enabled to talk it out and stop blaming myself. I know it might sound as if I am blaming others (including the Lord), but my frustration is because some others do not appear to understand the torment I am in. I am confident in what I know spiritually, but I am still tortured by my earthly mind.

One of the more repulsive methods of torture used in the old days was to strap a prisoner face to face to a rotting corpse, or a dying man. Paul the apostle actually had to endure this particular delicacy and he paints a vivid picture of what it feels like for many believers. As I explained previously I feel as if I have a dual personality, and this is true to a certain extent because the renewed and vibrant spiritual character within me is still strapped to the dying old woman, my fleshly, earthbound personality. This rotting character is now starting to really stink and catch in my throat; it really is time to let go.

I *am* letting go, this is why I am seeing a therapist. Each day I shed a little more of that muck which has hung around for much too long. I have realised how important it is to deal with the past, with any ingrained bitterness or grief or anger which has developed and festered from past experiences. If we don't do this we can become bitter to such an extent that there is no remedy, the bitterness eats away at any goodness that is left in us and we can become sour and distasteful and in extreme, downright obnoxious. I can see this in people I have known, and it is sad because they cannot see it in themselves, but occasionally it rises to the surface and causes a stink. I experienced this myself. I know I allowed the bitterness and hurt within me to spill over and hurt people who were trying to help me and for this I am very sorry. The Word describes it as 'the bitterness through which many are defiled' (Hebrews 12:15). Thankfully those who have helped and supported me will be recompensed and rewarded for their efforts, and this applies to all who have helped others. The Father has missed nothing.

The danger with bitterness is that left unchecked, it infects others too. Thankfully I was prevented from going too far down this road and I keep quiet now as often as I can, rather than stoop down to that level. I feel nauseous thinking about it. I could have been a victim but, thankfully, I am not... I am a true daughter of God, He has made me a true daughter of God and He has saved me from falling to that level and falling from His grace. What I mean by this is that there does come a point where His grace is no longer available to us, if we can no longer accept that there is crap inside us, if we ignore it and say, 'it's nothing'. It most definitely *is something.* Pretence, an act, doesn't cut it with the Lord. The heart has to be genuine. Belief/a good heart has to be genuine.

What is important ultimately is that we admit our faults and destructive thoughts to Him. *Something* generally causes us to become bitter, if it is not faced up to; if we do not fess up to ourselves, never mind to Him. He won't be angry. He is never angry with honesty and you can tell Him anything; nothing can shock God. It is the bitterness that can develop and grow as a result of keeping our troubles hidden and suppressed within us that spoils us as people in His sight, not the things we do. Bitterness left unchecked causes wars, in extreme.

God is love and we all need love to thrive. Sadly, some people never learn what true love is, so they can never show it or know how to accept it. Sometimes love is not reciprocated but abused, and this causes us to fear ever letting down our barriers and risk leaving ourselves vulnerable to more hurt. But love is the one thing that will remain in us for eternity, from this life. Love is the tie or glue that binds us. This book is a declaration of His love to those who are ready to accept that love, and it is given for those who need it and will respect and treasure it. There is nothing to fear from His love. His love for me is, I now see, what has carried me through everything. He has bound me to Himself with it and for that I will be eternally thankful.

Unfortunately I still blame myself for many things, but I will learn to live and love again and feel safe again around other people. I am still in survival mode because I am still fragile; the Lord and the Father know. But I also know I am safe in Their hands and with the Holy Spirit, who is surrounding me. When I like myself and can accept once more that this is who I am and He has made me this way for His purposes and I do not need the approval of those who might criticise me or try to control me, then I will be able to move on (completing this book, against all odds, is part of the process.)

If you are battling in your own mind to know if He accepts you as you are, this book should help you to understand that He does accept you and loves you, exactly as you are, despite what others might think. At least I do still retain a shred of that confidence, more than I realise... remember, I am slow to catch on, but don't dismiss me for that.

He is greater/stronger than our hearts and minds (1 John 3:20-22 if our heart condemns us, God is greater than our heart, and knows all things.) He is the final word. We can trust Him. He is the door to a much better life, with real love, to come.

⋆ ⋆ ⋆ ⋆ ⋆

The Jewish patriarch Abraham understood what it feels like to be filled with dark thoughts (as did Job and King David (Psalm 38:8 *I have roared because of the disquietness of my heart...the light of my eyes is gone from me.* Sounds familiar? Depression is not unusual, or a new thing). The Lord appeared to Abram and made a significant promise to Him regarding the nation that would come out of him (it looked impossible because he was an old man and his wife, Sarai, was past child bearing age, but Abram believed God and he was rewarded for his faith/belief. After the promise was given Abraham (the new name the Lord gave him, for his renewed life with God) fell asleep and had a terrifying waking nightmare, 'a horror of great darkness' (Genesis 15) and he had to push the dark thoughts aside several times throughout the night. He was shown that the promised seed or family would be afflicted or looked down upon by other nations for four hundred years and that eventually they would come out of this dreadful time with great substance (wealth), which was fulfilled when the Children of Israel went to Egypt. The Jews were originally called the children of Israel. Israel was Abraham's only son, who himself went on to have twelve sons and several daughters. Abraham had another son, Ishmael, by Sarah's maid and this is why others also claim Abraham as their father, but they are not of the promised line... sorry, guys! But, it doesn't matter anymore because the Lord has provided another, universally available, way! For the rest of us our earthly heritage/line has no bearing in the life to come. For the Jews it is a slightly different matter because He will appear to them in the context of their Jewish heritage, in a final mission to save them also, before this world comes to its final End.

Abram was also told that they would be afflicted, held captive again, which ended when Moses was chosen to lead them out of Egypt and into the wilderness, where they wandered for forty years. This has been the case historically for the Jews on and off ever since, which could have ended forever if they had accepted Jesus as the One sent to be their Messiah and Saviour. But there is a time of terrible tribulation followed by an experience and blessing which will come, even for the Jews, before He comes for them in the very last era of God's plan for mankind on this earth. (A very brief explanation; this is not supposed to be a history lesson, it is a promise of good things to come! But I have expanded on this later on in the book.)

This is a very basic explanation, but from it you should get my original point that even when we know Him we are not excluded from terrifying thoughts and nightmares, if we trust God, eventually He will reward us with great eternal wealth and substance. That is one of His promises to those of us who can believe now. The rewards for perseverance will be great. And even if you feel that you cannot hold on, He is holding on to you and He will not let go and His love will save you from being lost forever. We will continue to make mistakes. We will still have our faults and do things that we regret, but He will not condemn or blame us; He knows that we are not perfect; we never can be as fleshly, carnal men and women. But we can take His strength and assurance and latch on to him and come to God and find a better, more rewarding way of life, and spiritual perfection, even in this life.

Interestingly the words 'mistake' and 'regret' cannot be found in the Bible. For some reason I had thought that the Lord said that He regretted flooding the earth in Noah's time, but then I remembered that He said that He was sorry that He had 'made man on the earth and it grieved Him at His heart' (Genesis 6:6) because during that time people were even more depraved and destructive than they are in this day and age. It must have grieved Him terribly to see His beautiful creation being abused so badly. No one respected God or His things or each other for that matter. They were self-indulgent in extreme. The only person with any conscience was Noah and it was because of him that God didn't wipe everyone out (only Noah's family were saved and frankly they weren't much better); the world has never been without His witness, even in the direst circumstances.

Previous to that one great flood, which covered the whole

earth, it had not rained on the earth. A dew came up every morning and the temperature on the earth was consistent throughout (it was a very different world). Can you imagine the ridicule Noah and his family suffered when he said that he was building an ark (a huge ship) because water was going to fall out of the sky until the whole earth was submerged because God was so pissed off with everyone? That bloke had guts. They had no idea what he was talking about, except they would have known that their defiance against God and His things was not acceptable; bad manners in extreme.

The Lord's promises to us at this time aren't much different. How can we begin to grasp what heaven will be like? It is largely beyond our experience. How can we believe in a God we have never physically seen? Thankfully the Holy Spirit works His work on our hearts and makes it possible. All that we have to do is take that first step and believe. That really is all that the Lord expects us to do.

It is not my part to argue the timelines and the history of the world and creation or whatever beginning others choose to believe. As far as I am concerned the Bible is the true account of Earth's early history (the stars and planets are for signs/messages) and the things to come, the things written in there are sufficient for us to know. I believe Him; it is as simple as that. He does not have to explain or excuse Himself. Time will eventually tell all. He is now looking forward and so must I and, as I already explained, I have no fear of death, no fear of Him, in the sense of being afraid of Him; it is sensible to fear what He is capable of; it is wise to fear the alternative, which is a lost eternity for rejecting the truth when it is delivered on a plate, when it is made clear in His grace. That to me is priceless and I have no desire to question His wisdom in the way that He has done anything. He is God and He is my friend. You may take the piss, if you like, but it will not change how I feel or stop me from spreading the word. I want to go 'home' and the sooner He comes for us the better. Things are bloody tough for me right now but my victory is in my labour, in this work for Him, and as a consequence for many others too, I trust. Things are definitely looking up! I have a strong feeling that some of you will also be relieved and quietly rejoicing that He has heard your cries for help.

CHAPTER 5

When we were taken out of the cult, the Lord advised me to write about my experiences and observations and the revelations that He has given me, as a record, as my witness to God and His Son, the Lord Jesus Christ and His Holy Spirit working in my life (and the life of my friends), which also includes the messages that He wants me to share with you. This is the content of my journals. They are a record or witness in themselves. I was told that a heavenly recorder is duplicating my journals and they will be referred to when those people included in them stand before Him to give account for their actions. And they are also evidence of the belief and trust of myself and others. I have 'memories' of previous lives when I have walked this earth and done this very same thing. This is almost too incredible for me to believe and grasp, and I know that the concept is rejected by some of my contemporaries, but these memories are as vivid as my memories of this life - more vivid in some instances.

Time and timing has massive significance in God's will for mankind. From the very beginning of this creation God established time as a feature of His plan, and we are familiar with, and limited to or restricted by, a 24 hour day timeline. The Father Himself has reserved the right to work within His own parameters (limits or boundaries), whenever He chooses. A day in His timeline can be several months or years; for example, these are the End days, the final chapter in the earth's history, and this period began soon after the Lord ascended to heaven. But, this period is rapidly coming to a close. (Clearly, while we are told that God created the world in seven days, these 'days' could realistically have been a combination of many thousands of years.)

The Lord has used time in a most unusual way to establish a quick way to send a message to my friend and daughter Chris and myself, and it has been a source of comfort to both of us, usually when we have needed it the most. In early 2011 Chris sent me a text which simply said, '12:34?', referring to the time, thinking that she had already explained to me that she had noticed that every day for at least a week she had glanced at the clock at this exact time. She hadn't told me about this previously, so I assumed that she was referring to a scripture reference and I checked it out and discovered that chapter 12, verse 34 occurs in all four gospels. No other book in the Bible has this reference. This simple 12:34 was the beginning of an amazing message of comfort and hope, and even though we can never remember every aspect of this detailed message, which we could not have imagined or made up ourselves (we are not that bright or calculating), every time we see that time reference, 12:34, we know He is with us.

Check it out! (Matthew 12:34) 'Out of the abundance (excess) of the heart (thoughts and feelings) the mouth speaks', meaning what comes out of our mouths generally reflects the thoughts that are going around in our head. V35 continues 'a good man generally speaks good things and an evil man speaks evil (= hurtful) things', but this gives a wholly wrong impression of what Jesus was saying to the Jewish spiritual leaders ('the generation of vipers', (vicious snakes!) who were especially cruel in their financial demands on the people). I have just learned that this word 'evil' also means pain and anguish as a result of our daily toil or struggles (to put food on the table etc), which puts a very different slant on what Jesus was saying. This pain or sadness or anguish that the common people felt at that time, in their struggle to make ends meet, was very similar to how many people are feeling financially, and therefore emotionally or psychologically, in this present day. Therefore what comes out of our mouths simply reflects the pressure that we are under in our lives (we call it moaning or complaining) but the Lord doesn't condemn us for that. He understands that it's sometimes very hard going, and He also understands that we need to talk about it and get it off our chests.

So, the first part of the message from 12:34 is simply that *He understands why we cannot always be happy,* especially in this present financial climate and as a result of all the other troubles going on in the world and in our daily lives.

(Mark 12:34): One of the scribes came to Jesus and asked Him which commandment was the most important. The Lord asked the scribe what he thought the answer was and the man basically replied that we should love God more than anyone or anything else and that this meant more to God than any 'good works' we might do to impress Him.

'When Jesus saw that he answered discreetly (showing that

the man had considered this carefully), Jesus said, 'You are not far from the kingdom of God'. The Lord was simply saying to the scribe, and to us, that we are near to Him if we love Him more than anything or anyone else. (Frankly, it's not difficult when you begin to know or learn what He is really like. He is the best that is for certain! He is more loving and kind and patient and caring etc than any human being. And He has seen us. And He has seen you also in your hour of need.)

Luke 12:34: 'Where your treasure is, there will your heart be also'.

Jesus was speaking to His 'little flock' on this occasion and showing us (and them) that while we may not have much treasure or money on this earth, *in heaven we are pretty wealthy* (and it is constantly adding up!) because we have not set our heart on worldly riches. Simple, really!

Finally (John 12:34) 'The Son of man must be lifted up'. At that time, the Lord was speaking about the fact that He would have to be lifted up on the cross. He was telling them what was going to happen to Him, as Jesus (the son of man, as a man) and what it would accomplish, ie the downfall of Satan and all people being drawn to God, and not only the Jews. For us there is an additional message and this, in effect, is the purpose of this book: *to lift the Lord Jesus Christ up, as He is now*, in His glorified form, in the sight of everyone who reads this book.

However, there was more to learn about the message contained in 12:34. Recently I was inspired to find out the meanings of the numbers and the combination of the numbers themselves (with the help of the work of Sir Robert Anderson:

Numbers in Scripture). And this is what it revealed:

1 = unity (of the Godhead = the Father, the Son and the Holy Spirit)

2 = there is another (= the enemy, the opposition) and this also relates to division and something different.

12 = God as Ruler/King and also governmental perfection

30 = a higher degree of divine order

3 = stands for that which is solid and real and complete and completely divinely perfect

4 = the number of man and God's creative works.

12:34 therefore encompasses time and scripture, ie God's declared word, through Jesus, the Lord, when He was a man on earth. It also reveals the unity of mind and purpose between God, our heavenly Father and His Son, the Lord Jesus Christ, and His Spirit (the power of God). It also reminds and warns us that there is another force at work among us, who is the enemy of all that is good and whose aim is to divide and separate;

But central in all this is the assurance that God is overall ruler and King and in that there is governmental perfection; an overall perfect power behind everything. And there is also a much higher degree of divine order to everything, despite how things very often appear.

God stands for or represents everything that is real and solid and complete and His creative works, which includes His plan for mankind, are utterly, fucking perfect!

Now there is absolutely no way that we could remember all these aspects to this message (the simple 12:34) when it is given, but when it is brought to our attention it should remind us that He is real and with us and He is in overall control, and this message is especially pertinent or lush when everything else around us seems to be falling apart and persuading us that He has forgotten us.

I could leave it at that. When I initially typed this I was only on chapter three, a perfect number scripturally. Now it is chapter five, the number of grace, and His everlasting grace is definitely with us. He is moving among us. I could leave it there but I can't, because this is only the beginning of The Message (and we need at least chapters 1, 2, 3 and 4... 5 (grace), 6 (?) and so on). But, if this is as much as you need, if this is how far you want to go; it is enough. Simply remember 12:34. This is a perfect, sound message. 1, 2, 3, 4, 5; even a young child can recite and remember this simple message, most probably in several languages. Praise the Lord for the little children; they are included.

CHAPTER 6

Almost every morning during the two years since I walked away from my home I have woken up and stepped outside for a while and waited for the Lord to speak. (Before this, when I wasn't ill, I would get up during the night, when I was strong enough, to spend time with the Lord, but now I am not so hard on myself.) I have a smoke when I go outside, but my real reason for being out there is to listen for Him. At some stage I am hoping that the penny will drop and I will realise that I can go out to see Him without a cigarette in my hand. Anyway, the point is, autumn, winter, spring and summer He is there, and every day the Father has said something or shown me something. How blessed, how privileged am I? Sometimes He will begin by showing me something; some examples are a discarded piece of plastic or toy, a stone or cloud in a recognisable shape, the birds in fight or mating or singing, the frog I told you about. Then, as I ponder and consider, I start to understand what He is saying. I have needed to hear Him every morning ('morning by morning He brings His judgments to light' or words to that effect, from somewhere in the Book of Psalms, I believe).

I was especially grateful for this daily guidance and reassurance at the beginning because we had broken away from everything we had known and trusted, even though much of it was a sham (but not a *complete* shambles, the Father and the Lord had Their eye on us the whole time!) Previous to this, as I already explained, we were guided mainly through the Word/the Bible, (the Lord Himself speaking in text) and through the Gifts of the Holy Spirit 'helped' by the bloke who was in charge, but he used God's word to his advantage and twisted it; that pile of dung made sure in a roundabout way that he had the last word. If we showed him what we had been given from the Bible and he wasn't happy with it, he would give his interpretation, which we were expected to follow (bastard!). It was therefore refreshing to be shown that the Father Himself can speak for Himself, or more to the point, that He wanted to speak for Himself - to me!

I have to be honest, I have rather taken this for granted. This morning I found myself not smoking my cigarette but thinking that I am sleeping a lot at the moment and talking in the Spirit (praying or speaking in tongues) to the Father and the Son, before They spoke to me, for a change. I should talk to Them more, using the Spirit because the Holy Spirit knows what we need; He knows exactly what to ask. The manifestation or evidence of the Spirit working in us is the ability to speak in different tongues or languages. Feel free to ask the Lord for this and then just open your mouth and see what comes out. It might take a few attempts and only be a couple of words but that's OK please don't stress about it; it will come, it will grow and develop; it isn't compulsory however.

When I know what to ask for, which I often do, I put it to Him and sometimes, as I have said already, They don't always respond straight away, which can be frustrating because patience is not my best asset. The Father is very gracious. He listens to me rambling on about how sad I am, how afraid I am, how lost I feel, how I cannot understand why He hasn't answered my big prayers or requests, etc. Occasionally (not often enough) I thank Him/Them, when I remember, for being there, for Their love, for everything He has done for me; He is amazing, so incredibly patient. I guess He just switches out for a bit because He already knows what I need or I am thinking before I do, but He does want to hear from me. He is like the best dad really. I get a lot of attention, considering how many children He has. He is patient because He *is* the best Father and in the same way that we expect our children to take what we do for granted, He understands that we take Him for granted. Like a child should be allowed to do.

I simply accept that He is much wiser and more capable than I am, than *we* are. I have no idea how He listens to us all, how He sees everything that is going and so-on; I cannot remember, so I simply accept it.

I have no real need to question it but I trust that if I need to understand something, anything, He will show me, or the Lord or the Holy Spirit will.

I have to say at this juncture that children today are expected to know too much, make decisions too early, be responsible at far too young an age in these progressive times. Some simply are not ready for such responsibility the minute they can talk. Whatever happened to allowing children to be children? There, I've said my piece.

However, getting back to what I was saying, He is patient,

thankfully, but this morning the Lord did show me that fellowship/conversation (friendship with God) has to be a two-way thing. I am not a child any more spiritually and He expects me to pull my weight and talk to Him with confidence, even if I don't exactly feel confident in the flesh or happy. I need to rejoice more in what He has achieved for me, for us, when I meet Him in the mornings.

Reading back through everything I have written so far has made me realise how much I have to be thankful to Him for. I do sing in the Spirit/in tongues and thank Him and talk to Him at other times, sometimes constantly and subconsciously. It's an unconscious thing, like breathing, but these times in the mornings are precious because that is when I am at my most vulnerable to attack (the crap in my head when I am waking up is unbelievably horrendous most mornings) and going to Him, to Them, is necessary for my sanity.

The Holy Spirit is a very useful tool for asking the Lord for the right things or rejoicing (He is not a 'tool', in the sense of the modern slang for the term, 'piece of work' of my day); He is a great help or Helper, in this respect. He has the right words and it involves very little effort on our part; I don't have to pretend to be happy, I simply have to be willing to trust Them.

Which brings me to the other issue of the day - sleep, or too much of it!

Sometimes we do 'sleep for sorrow'; the mind has this brilliant capacity to shut the thoughts and the body down when it needs to conserve or recharge energy for the body and mind to repair itself or avoid something. Sometimes life itself becomes too much for the mind to handle, especially in stress situations.

Very often we might try to fight through, to overcome, but the fight and flight mechanism of the brain is sleep. If we are physically ill we need to sleep more than at other times to let the body redirect its resources to the areas which need repairing, and it is the same for the benefit of the mind. I would feel guilty about the amount of sleep that I am getting, except the Lord said, 'He gives His beloved sleep'. God knows best how to help me cope in these difficult times. And I am very fortunate to have a bed and a room in which to do so, even though I do not have a home of my own yet. When the body is recharged the mind is better able to process information, especially the hard stuff. What I am saying is that we should not feel guilty about sleeping, when we need to (unless we know that we are just plain lazy). On other occasions we might simply be sleeping through the terrible storm of opposition, trusting the Father, as the Lord did in the boat (Mark 4:37 etc.)

I seem to have digressed, but I trust that what I have had to say has been necessary for someone.

Time to move on.

CHAPTER 7

One of the very first personal messages was given to me in November 2010,That year it was apparently the coldest, crispest winter in 100 years and a very happy time for me. The Lord reminded me of my ultimate purpose or calling in His will, from Luke 4:18,19: 'The Spirit of the Lord is upon me... to preach the acceptable year of the Lord', ie to herald or proclaim the Lord's second coming, His return to take us Home, in His glorified form, as He is now: Lord of lords, King of kings.

(v21) 'This day (in November 2010) is this scripture fulfilled in your ears.' My problem now is how much of what He has said to me I need to share with others. If I had the time I would share most of it, except for the most intimate revelations, but realistically I must keep it fairly brief and confine myself to the messages from God to you, Reader, messages relating to His coming. That simplifies things! As you can see I have not managed to do this so far, so it is unlikely that I will do it in the following chapters. However, the main message is that He is inviting all who can hear to expect His coming. We are now in the 'acceptable year (time/era) of the Lord'.

My part, as far as I can see, is the same as that of John (the baptist), who heralded or came a few months before the Lord to announce His first coming, as the Messiah of the Jews, but my ministry extends to reinforce Jesus' own teachings or ministry: 'The Spirit of the Lord (God) is upon me, because He has anointed me to preach the gospel to the poor; He has sent me to heal the broken hearted, to preach deliverance to the captives, and recovering of sight to the blind, to set at liberty them that are bruised, to preach the acceptable (accepted or approved for receiving) year of the Lord.'

When Jesus Himself quoted these words from the book of Isaiah, the people who were there struggled to accept that He was anyone other than Joseph's son, even though 'they wondered at the gracious words which came out of His mouth'. The rulers of the synagogues were downright angry; they hated Him, mainly because they could see that His teaching had the potential to destroy their livelihood. They were doing very nicely, thank you, in their control over His people, by exploiting the Law which He gave to keep them safe and separate, until His arrival.

The Lord was not fazed. He realised that very few would acknowledge who He really was; God's Son, their Messiah, because He was an ordinary guy and not exactly an attractive one. Outwardly He was a plain, hook-nosed Jew from a poor family (nothing like He is portrayed in all the great paintings). He also knew that even though He would die for them, at their hand (with the help of the Romans), there were some, a few, who would accept Him and be glad of His words and that ultimately His ministry and purpose was more far reaching than the Jews understood (even though it was prophesied in their writings/scriptures).

I trust that some readers will most definitely be happy to

hear the messages that I have been given, but I am no stranger to rejection and I know that some will mock me and wind me up. But I mustn't be a pessimist, all the signs are good and there are people who are most certainly crying to God for help and advice, a sign; and want to know the truth, otherwise what would be the point? Others are simply waiting and perhaps do not even realise it. He is coming for us soon; this is the bottom line, so those of us who take this seriously need have no real worries. This life and its troubles are temporary. Eternity is a very different matter, and I know where I would prefer to spend it.

Which brings me, conveniently, to my next reference from my Journal dated 12th November 2010: After the Lord's body was taken down from the cross it was put in a tomb and the door was sealed. I don't intend to give a blow by blow account of the exact events and comings and goings from the tomb and the garden where they put His body, as these details are available for you to read for yourself in the closing chapters of the gospels (Matthew, Mark, Luke and John's accounts of these events). However there are one or two details which are relevant and necessary for proper understanding.

The two Marys; the Mary who is often referred to as Mary Magdalene, and 'the other Mary' (the woman chosen to be His birth mother) sat and watched one of His disciples, a rich man called Joseph make all the necessary preparations and provision; he laid the Lord's body in his own new tomb and sealed it, with an enormous stone. Eventually the women went home but they returned several days later to the sepulchre and at some point during the events of the days after the Lord had died and gone down to hell and risen again, Peter and John had also visited the grave and finding it empty had run off to tell the other disciples.

However, the two Marys returned to find there had been an earthquake, which had moved the great stone which was now lying to one side at the opening of the grave and an angel was sitting on it. We are told, 'his countenance was like lightening...' Interestingly, this refers to the way the angel was staring or gazing at the empty sepulchre in astonishment. He was staring in wide-eyed amazement at what Jesus (the man) had done by faith (belief in and obedience to His Father's will). As a man He had actually come back from hell and retrieved or gone back into His earthly body and walked into heaven and had now returned to speak with His disciples before finally ascending to be with His Father forever. The angels, who are servants and messengers of God, appear not to have been aware of this chain of events in advance or, if they were, they did not believe it was possible.

'...and his (the angel's) clothing was white as snow'. His clothes were like snow, luminous white and like snow in the sense that it cannot be grasped as it falls, it is empty and not solid. The keepers who worked in the garden were so afraid when they saw him that they had collapsed in fear, but the women evidently stood their ground because the angel spoke to them and said, ' Don't be afraid of me; FOR I KNOW THAT YOU SEEK JESUS, who was crucified. He is not here; for He is risen... come and see the place where the Lord was laid and then go and tell His disciples that He is risen from the dead; and He has gone ahead of you into Galilee, where you will see Him' and he concluded with the words, 'There (or lo), I have told you'. It is almost as if the angel was as shocked as they were and was glad to have got his part in this out of the way.

The angel advised the women that the risen Lord (Jesus) was pushing on, forward and ahead of them to Galilee (which is a region of Palestine and regarded at the time, as it is now, as the heathen circle or circuit because they were not of the chosen line). Anywhere outside of Israel would have been considered to be heathen territory and yet this was the direction that the Lord was pressing on towards, He was moving in the direction of the world in general and advising His disciples to follow Him there. His ministry to the Jews was more or less over for the time being.

There were just a few more radical or fanatical Jews, extremists, who would be converted to the new way. In the new dispensation of grace for all, the apostle Paul was the first of the new wave. Paul (= pause, stop, restrain; he was literally stopped in his tracks) was originally called Saul (=request, demand, ask; Saul was an angry man) but the Lord changed his name to Paul. Also, if you are interested, the early believers/Christians were called Followers of the Way.

The point from this account which I feel is relevant as I write, is that He knows and I know that some of you 'seek Jesus'; seeking something...answers. Some of you are looking to Him and asking for help, advice; something tangible, something real (some of you are probably angry too, doing your best to suppress your anger and confusion; putting on a face.). And here He is; this is His answer. He is asking you to pause and stop going on without Him and then push on forward with His support to His appearing. I too am pressing forward, completing my work on this earth, in preparation for His coming. I can't bloody wait.

I find it comforting that He appeared to Mary Magdalene first. Mary M had gone back to the garden during the night, which is probably when He appeared to her, and then she returned again with the other Mary in the morning and this is why the two women weren't afraid of the angel when they saw him. Clearly the Lord loved Mary M and did not want her to be upset and distressed for too long. She was the one He chose to advise the disciples that He had come back to see them all. She was a gutsy woman, because it would have been a very daunting task for a woman in those times to advise men; as it can still be in some cases in this modern age. (message in for me through the Radio: 'Light up, light up, as if you have a choice, even if you cannot hear My voice, I'll be right beside you dear' Snow Patrol) This, and Jesus reappearing to Mary M first, puts into perspective the respect that the Lord has for women spiritually, and the place we hold in God's heart, but astonishingly some men appear to regard those of us who love Him with suspicion and some contempt. Incredible, really! I am not very well read on Jewish etiquette regarding women, but from what I can tell, especially from the Bible accounts, Jewish women are respected, especially by the less fanatical sector, although females might still be kept separate from the men in Temple worship. As believers and followers of the new way, we now approach God, men and women, as individuals, as priests in our own right. Temple worship is now no longer relevant. To any Jews out there who might be reading this, 'Sorry, guys! You missed Him the last time He came to earth but there is still time, however, a brief window, to change your mind, your way of thinking; clean out your ears and come to Him with an open heart.' It is a level playing field at the moment. We are in the dispensation of Grace and there is grace in abundance, but when He comes again to earth as Ruler and King (after His coming for believers, the followers of His Way I might add, and we are safely home); when He comes back to earth to Rule it will be very different state of affairs; He will be the *only* Ruler on earth and no one will challenge Him. I would suggest that if you do not believe me that you read your scriptures, particularly the writings of the Moses and the other prophets, as it is all in there; the writing is on the wall (perhaps the wailing wall), so to speak.

* * * * *

You might like to read the account of Mary's initial reunion with the risen Lord, her Master, in John's Gospel, chapter 20; it is very moving, and also His subsequent reunions with the disciples.

We are told that Jesus cast seven devils out of Mary and I believe Mary might be the woman whom the Lord saved from a severe beating when the religious fanatics brought her to Him, accusing her of screwing around basically; virtually accusing her of being a prostitute, and this is why she loved Him so much. (I cannot prove this because this particular woman is not given a name in the account but I suspect it could possibly be Mary M.) As cool as you like, the Lord, who was squatting on the dusty ground when the men brought her to Him, started to draw in the dust with a stick and asked those of them who had no sin and had never made any mistakes to throw the first stone. It seems incredible that this kind of barbaric scene can be witnessed in countries where the stoning of women is still condoned and practised, in the name of God, and women are regarded with utter contempt and of less value than sheep and dogs. Whoever this woman was, she did not deserve this treatment in God's name.

The Lord/God loves women. In His sight we are spiritually and socially and intellectually equal. The only difference is that, in the main, we are physically not as strong. In every other sense we are equal to men. Make no mistake, God expects men to be kind to women and women to be kind to men. There will be no mercy for anyone who has been arrogant and consequently physically or mentally abusive to another, whether it is towards a man or a woman or a child. Paul advised in his letter to the believers in Ephesus; husbands should love and cherish their wives and that the wives should respect their husbands. Personally I feel we should love and respect each other. We all thrive on love, as I observed earlier. (Realistically, not all women deserve this respect and neither do some men. Common sense has to prevail.)

Today I am strangely calm. Last night I realised that it is time to 'own' my faith again; to regain my confidence in Him and also in my own belief and excitement and the calm joy in Him, which I strongly felt when we broke away from our oppressor (in 2010 J). I cannot really explain the circumstances of why my joy and confidence were rattled and severely undermined because if I do I would also betray my friends. This has been a learning curve for all of us and we have all had our 'demons' to face and deal with - or not, whatever the case may be. Everyone has their own way of listening to the Lord and coping with events and moving forward. We all have a place, a part to fulfil in His will. The essential factor is, we all love Him and He loves us. The main thing for me is I have regained my own peace and confidence. And I must determine to hold on to them this time. 'Come on Nik, dry your eyes love, the bad times are over for you' is more or less what He said. I am so privileged to know Him; my Lord, our Lord. Things aren't entirely right yet, though I desperately wish they were.

I am aware that I need to ask more often for the support of the Holy Spirit to maintain my confidence. I am representing Him and I know that the Lord wants me to be completely open and outspoken ('light up, light up!') and at times be blunt, to speak boldly, as the prophets of old did. To do this with my confidence dismantled, as it has been, requires a touch from Him - several, in fact. A couple of jugs full of the Holy Spirit would do nicely at the moment, thanks Lord!

CHAPTER 8

Early in 2011 I was given the message. As I already explained, it is not essentially new but is based on a combination of things that the Lord and others said. It's very straightforward and simple and it is what it is.

All of a sudden my enthusiasm has bombed; self-condemnation and doubt have reared their ugly heads again. (Rollercoaster, init? Or Rollincoaster, considering my surname). I need to think about this carefully. Frankly, I'm confused. My problem is... I do tend to listen too much to criticism and opinions and crap from others. This can't be avoided, of course, unless I become a monk, and to do that I'd have to get a sex change first, which would involve far too much pain and mess and effort. My mouthy rebellious (some might say immature) alter ego is screaming to be let loose. I am living in a so very polite and prim and proper environment at the moment and it's doing my bleeding head in; we're all on our best behaviour, for good reason, I might add. I mustn't rise to the provocation and let my tongue loose, but the Oppo is jabbing at me pretty hard and that's probably because the Father has assured me yet again (He is *sooo* patient and I'm such an idiot at times) that a change is on its way and that I just have to stay put and keep my mouth shut and watch Him work. Interesting. Exciting. Intriguing... frustrating. Hopefully it will soon be time to really shine! More patience for me, but I've got much to be thankful for, as you must agree. Sometimes I am a miserable whining spaz (suck it in, woman!)

Now I've got all that crap off my chest, I can focus again. This has to be better than skewering somebody with a sharp stick (several people spring to mind). Perhaps not as satisfying, but the repercussions are much less damaging (I'm only joking - kind of!). Deep breath. Apologies, people; I'm having a bad attack of the mental mentals. If I continue typing I shall be talking in riddles. I hate myself sometimes. OK, pressing forward...

Why does this keep happening to me? I actually know the answer – it is brain overload (and I am still defragging, clearing out all the past muck; I shouldn't be so tough on myself!) The responsibility of writing this and getting it right is very nearly killing me, so I have to do a back flip (figuratively speaking), every now and again. It just seems I am doing it more 'now' than 'again'. Good job He understands; I'm guessing the angels are shaking their heads and saying, 'He must know what He's doing; He *does* know what He's doing': He has 'chosen the weak things of this world to confound the mighty... and things which are despised He has chosen, to bring to nothing the things that are (respected and valued by the know- it-alls and the rich etc, of this world -1 Corinthians 1 verses 27-29. His reasoning behind this is so that when we come to Him, we are not telling Him how 'good and great' *we* are. If we know we are nothing in this life, but we also know He loves us all the same and has prepared an amazing life for us in the next, we are pretty much bombproof and I, for one, am very grateful to Him for what He has done. I long for the next life.

It is very comforting to know how close by He is because the Oppo weaves a pretty tangled web to get through, at times and we have to go through the darkness to reach the light because, we are told, God lives/dwells in the centre of the thick darkness. Moses went up the mountain and up to where the clouds were dark and dense to where God was and I have often wondered what this means in respect of our experience/life now, as believers. As I am typing those words in I can see that a basic meaning is that without God, humans are darkness, if His light is not switched on, but His light is there deep within most people, even when we are not aware of it. And the world itself is a dark place without His light; spiritually and in a physical sense. He made the light, in fact it was one of the first things He put in place; there is a reason for that, something to do with physics (which I am not hot on but I recall being told that He made everything from the components of light), but it isn't essential for us to understand that. I said that already but all these things are repeated for a reason.

Unfortunately, we have to battle to get through the darkness which can feel so overwhelming in order to see Him within ourselves; to feel His presence. (23rd August 2012 – Personally today I feel as if I have climbed a huge mountain and all I appear to have found at the top is darkness. Maybe I have to wait for my eyes to adjust or for the clouds to clear. Or maybe just listen. I feel sick and need to shake this overpowering malaise/sadness, which plagues me. The Father said this morning that I am who I am and I've got balls!

Evidently He knows me a lot better than I do. It would have been my eldest son's birthday today.)

I'm not sure I'm too keen on the wording; *thick* darkness, as in dense or stupid... or maybe Solomon was right on this occasion too (1 Kings 8:12) because we are very often *thick* (as in stupid or dim), especially if we do not believe in God. He is no different to us, truly HE isn't (except He is never *dim.* dark maybe, silent, but never dim). This might seem like nonsense to you, it possibly is (are you confounded yet? I do hope not, unless you are beginning to think like Him, and then maybe you will understand. But don't worry if you don't, there is time yet. I'm just playing with the words, because my head is upset, but it's all true, nevertheless).

(25th October 12 – I have recently read a book called *The Woman who Went to Bed for a Year* by Sue Townsend, about a woman who retreated to her bed in an attempt to make sense of her life. It is marketed as 'a glorious laugh out loud' but, although there are some funny observations, it is ostensibly incredibly sad. The main character's retreat from the world and her family is what I, and many others, feel they need to do, in order to escape from the overwhelming feelings of low self-worth and confusion. In the end she asks to be barricaded in to her room and she slowly starves to death but, before this happens, her ageing mother and her only remaining friend break the door down and bathe her and carry her to the comfort of the sofa, in front of a log fire. The concluding words are spoken by the woman, Eva (cannot be coincidence; Eve was the first woman), 'It's kindness, isn't it? Simple kindness.'

Simple kindness is akin to love and is incredibly important.

Those who have never experienced mental trauma of any description cannot understand how important it is to show those who are suffering; the smallest kindness; even if it is just a few kind words. Mental illness is so very isolating. *Not Shambles: Divine Intention* is a few sincere, kind words, with a promise of good things to come, and I trust that you can see this.

Tuned in to the radio... 'Another day in the life of me... can anybody hear me? Hello, hello, can you hear me?' I have no idea who is singing this but it is very appropriate because I am thinking, 'is anyone actually still listening/reading? Can I actually continue to believe that this is all true?' I feel lonely and isolated and in despair.

But this brings me very nicely to 'the nail in the sure place'; Thank you for reminding me, Holy Spirit.

In early 2011 a friend and I were sent by the Lord on a drive along the south coast of England. We had no idea where we were headed, but knew we should follow the signs. Not the conventional road signs but markers along the way, instructions via messages on the side of the road; on billboards, on the sides of lorries, place names. It was an indulgence on a shoestring but we had a blast and it was a prequel to the trip to Europe (with another friend). This might not seem unusual or particularly daring, but for us it was a huge step because we had been repressed and controlled for so long. It was part of the breaking-free process. Eventually, my mate and I ended up in Eastbourne, where I was assured that I had established my own 'nail in a sure place'; I had made it to the top and now had a firm nail to which I could attach myself and keep climbing to the heights of heaven. The Lord, Jesus, is that nail.

My Mum explained that for years she had had a recurring dream. She was in Eastbourne (somewhere she had never visited) and she and my Dad were looking for somewhere to stay. A guy led them around to the back of a building where there were many stairs to climb, but they never made it to the top before she woke up and the going was too hard. I have the nail now Mum, I understand; He has enabled me to reach the top, we have the most incredible place to stay and he will lift you up; no worries.

A calm confidence has once again replaced the frustrated madness of yesterday... phew! As you know I habitually get up early in order to wake up slowly and, as I am very nearly always greeted by a barrage of abuse and conflict (from my own mind, provoked and poked by the Oppo, and only rarely from anyone else these days... bonus), I need that time to at least attempt to tune in to His mind or His way of thinking and make sense of the garbage that grinds me down. As I believe I already explained, the Holy Spirit usually shows me something or reminds me of something which starts the process of healing for the day. (Are we going around in circles, or is it just me? I asked you to join me, and this is my life. 'Please make a way for me to get off this tedious ride soon, Lord!')

Anyway, the thought for this particular morning was, 'the early bird catches the worm' to settle my mind regarding a promise I was given some time ago. Too long ago it seems; it is a euphemism for so many things but sadly not the innuendo that will initially spring to some deliciously filthy minds - or perhaps not. I feel greatly encouraged, however, to know that I am still alive in that respect. Enough on that... anyway, moving on! There are plenty of other books to titillate and stir your passion, so to speak. I have other things to tell you. I must add that sex done properly is vital and fucking lovely, or can be, even if it is only DIY, but the more personal details of my inner and outer workings are not for everyone's ears and eyes. I have to retain some mystery about my sexual urges and also regarding my own personal revelation (I will have good sex in heaven with someone and hopefully again in this life).

Sunday 19th continues: or began to be more precise, with thoughts of how I do not enjoy having a womanly shape, preferring to stay super skinny, because I do not want to be considered available and I don't like myself and would like to be invisible, which is sad. It is a mystery to me why men can assume when a woman is unattached and shapely and well turned out that she is looking for sex or a partner or that she is up for anything. I have to fight the desire to shag someone; I have needs, but I must be strong and resist. I am worth more than a quickie; been there, done that! Not that I mind a bit of banter, a laugh and a some ribbing, but I hate to be considered to be desperate, when I certainly am not, and neither do I look like a tart. If I was a prostitute, I would be honest about it, and I cannot say that the thought hasn't briefly crossed my mind, but I'm too old now anyway. I could pull a wealthy man if I set my mind to it but that is just prostitution in a fancy wrapper. But it has crossed my mind; I would be lying if I said it hadn't. When needs must, we sometimes are forced to consider doing things that we would otherwise reject. After all, I was made to feel like a whore by my abuser and my feeling of self-worth was so damaged and scarred that it did not seem inconceivable. A means to an end... but a *dead* end, ultimately. God has promised to always make a way; He will continue to support me. I have played the field in my youth, with a few one-night stands, but that doesn't diminish me as a person, it simply means I have a good sexual appetite. (I *love* sex; dirty, rough sex... too much information. Radio: 'I'm not a saint, I'm not a sinner but I don't care cos I'm getting thinner. I don't know what to think any more' Funny ha ha, Lord! Perhaps I should get laid again... I need to finish the book, then...maybe I'll get lucky.)

Looking back now I realise that some of it, sleeping around when I was younger, was rebellion against my circumstances, a strange warped way of validating myself, of taking control (oddly enough). After the deceitful sexual abuse I have suffered and two broken marriages, it is astonishing that I can even consider ever having sex or making love again. Thankfully my sense of self is still intact in some respects. These sorts of thoughts precipitate the degenerating spiral of feelings of low self-worth and this can very rapidly escalate to the point where I would seriously consider ending it all. So, I have learned to get up, to get out of the house and walk, or sit, and listen for His voice, His advice, which comes through lyrics and signs and *positive* memories regarding His continual presence and support in my life. The battle to hold on to the truth hardly ever stops, but I can at least limit the damage, by doing my best not to entertain or feed the negative thoughts. He is my main addiction, the loudest voice or influence in my life, and it is this that has saved me from ending it all or turning to drink or drugs for support, in any significant and damaging way. Without His constant presence in my life I would certainly have travelled down one of those incredibly sad dead end roads. I understand why it happens and so does He; life can be fucking totally unbearable; it is never too late to turn things around.

This morning, as I was walking and talking to Him (all Three of Them that is... the collective name 'God' sounds so harsh, even though They are God*. It's no different, I suppose to disliking my own name), but, staying focused and away from the verbals (verbal d and v)) and keeping to the point, I caught sight of a sign on the side of the road which I have not noticed previously 'No Cold Calling Zone', but I read it as No Cold Zoning. For me this was a short sharp reminder not to avoid love or accepting love, and the warmth of this emotion. As soon as I start to feel vulnerable, my barriers go up and my heart becomes cold as stone... no zoning out into that cold zone again, missus! I love to love, as the song goes, and I need to learn how it feels to be loved, without fear of repercussions. Love is such a precious thing, and strangely I do not feel worthy of it. Thankfully His love for us is not based on whether we are worthy or not; it is a free gift. I marvel that He loves me but I am very glad that He does.

During my break from typing I was considering whether you want or are interested in a blow by blow account of my day or my thought processes (too much verbals and not enough sex action...sexual frustration...aargh!). But, I guess in this age of chat sites and blogs and the large public appetite for soaps (me included, if and when I have time), it is equally significant that I should show you a real life with the Lord, warts and nearly all.

FOOTNOTE *Lord of hosts is one of my personal favourites: 'hosts' simply means many or multitudes, an army of people... He has many followers, on earth and in heaven, despite how it can appear; we are not walking or fighting alone.

You cannot help but have noticed that knowing Him is not a cure-all, in the sense that all your problems will suddenly magically disappear -I wish. The advantage of knowing Him, apart from the fact that death has lost its sting, is that you always have a best friend (but not a fuck buddy), who always understands and will never leave you or let you down if you trust Him, even if for some reason we lose our faith, God knows it has happened to me more than once. He is there to pick up the pieces when we turn back to Him; God is amazing.

Sometimes, as I have already shown, I wonder how much more I can take, how many more knockbacks? How much longer must I wait for some respite? Why are certain promises delayed? But, from experience, I know emphatically that He has always looked after me. I have known bounty and leanness: I have been comfortable and wanting for nothing and I have now got virtually nothing, but I have never been totally destitute. That is the only real significant difference between me and some of you (I know many *do* already believe in the truth but the Lord is making some things a bit clearer perhaps) and that saving grace is solely down to having God in my life. At this present time I have no means of supporting myself. I am essentially like you in many other ways; *He* is more like you, He is every man and woman, in that He knows us, understands us because the Lord, Jesus Himself, had a broad experience of life. It might sound vain and arrogant to some that I consider myself, my own experience of life, in the same context as Jesus' own*

I have had to experience many things that by choice I would have avoided. A minor example is that I detest having

FOOTNOTE *I have heard it called a Messiah complex.. the person who said it wasn't really bitter! Bitter as a lemon, he was a lemon), but I have worked hard for my confidence.

to continue to live on the charity of others, especially friends and including the state, but I am thankful that the provision is available and knowing that the provision is actually His undertaking removes any guilt I might feel, even though being dependent on others can be scary and means I do sometimes feel very vulnerable and insecure. I am not equipped in any shape or form to survive in the world on my own.

Deep down I know that the kind friend He has chosen to give me shelter and a safe place to sleep for now is genuine when he says I am secure with them. Nevertheless, it is just one of the humiliating indignities that I am forced to suffer, for several reasons, until the change comes. Realistically, I cannot be 100% certain that this friend won't let me down (I know he would never deliberately hurt me but we are all fallible, we all fail sometimes) but I do know that the Lord can't let me down... ever! That doesn't mean to say that I don't occasionally have doubts even about the very existence of God; trusting someone you have only ever actually seen in a fleeting vision, even when they bombard you with signs and messages of assurance that have no other earthly explanation, can be testing, but it *has* to be Him, simply owing to the consistency and quantity of these messages and His unfailing care. He meets my needs (but not my wants) every day. I am very blessed or fortunate, as some people live their lives trusting Him, hoping in Him, without any real proof. Good effort, guys! I mean that. I admire and respect you immensely. Others of you survive entirely on your own... incredible. For you the point of this revelation is that there is a reward prepared for you if you can accept it.

However, I understand that I have to know life and how it

feels to mistrust and trust, to such extreme degrees, otherwise how could I advise and write to you, Reader, with any authority or conviction, how could some of you be expected to listen and consider any of these truths – especially The Messages, His message to you/us all. (I am not deliberately delaying sharing the specific message, it is out of my control and I suspect it might come at the very end and it is His word to you that will surely shine out in conclusion. Be patient therefore, or at least try not to turn to the last few pages to find out. It is worth the wait... says she who is getting very impatient to see the fulfilment of His promises. I believe the right word is *thick*; I am a dumb ass at times.)

Speaking of change (wasn't I?) I had a few extra bevvies last night, while I was playing skittles. I continued my walk (and morning cogitations on that morning, not the 27th), as I very often do, to Welcome Break, bought a coffee and sat down to write, asking for advice, as my thoughts were still in a knot. As I put my hand into my bag to get my pen I pulled out a fragment of shopping list, which said 'filters/change' and 'sun bed'. That was His answer. Filters = learn to filter out the harmful crap; Change = a change will come, it always does eventually and He has promised over and over that this next change will be for the better. Finally sun - we in the UK could all do with some of that but there is more to this in my case, as I will explain in a minute; bed = don't lose sleep over anything, sleep is necessary. Pretty simple really, but you have to be willing to see these things, to hear His voice in such seemingly innocuous and insignificant ways. I can make today's message even more simple: filter out the crap, make a change to the way I think (or whatever), while I wait for the change He has promised, try and enjoy a bit of sun (get out in the fresh air) and then bed. It's all that is necessary for now (apart from the typing that is and food, of course). Takes the stress out of everything. He's not stressing so I don't need to either. I hope I can hang on to this one, for a few days at least! I need to get strong again, physically and psychologically. There will be work to do, when the **major change** eventually happens. (Major Change deserves a salute!)

The sun of righteousness:

Malachi 4:1,2: *For, behold* (understand for certain), *the day comes, that shall burn as an oven: and all the proud* (arrogant), yeah, *and all that do wickedly* (do things that are morally wrong or violate another human being, or deliberately make trouble and harbour trouble in their' hearts and provoke strife and discord), *shall be stubble* (like dry straw): *and* ***the day that is coming*** *shall burn them up, says the Lord* (there is a cut off point, God will only turn a blind eye to these wicked people, these tormentors who thrive on hurting and controlling other people who have good hearts; He will give them what they deserve... which is what they have done to others... magnified beyond anything we can imagine. Their anger and spite and hatred will turn in on themselves, because there will be no one else around to aim it at; and this will go on and on forever, for all eternity. *It shall leave them neither root nor branch...* which means their damaging effects will not last or stay with their victims, therefore take comfort my friends if you are being bullied or oppressed in any way. The day of vengeance and justice is fast approaching: God has not missed a thing; He sees everything. I *have* to believe in His justice, not only for my sake but because I have seen many times the effects of the loneliness and despair of the crushing isolation that such bullies create in the lives of their victims. It pisses me off big time! It makes my blood boil. Everyone knows someone who has suffered bullying in some form; Jesus was one of them and therefore His Father (and our Father) is not going to let that one pass unrequited indefinitely, that's for sure.

A whirlwind has gone forth, this is the last time or final era in God's plan, and there is going to be much confusion and upheaval in the world, but for those who can look to Him there will be peace and assurance. This is it! Even for those of you who do not even realise that you need Him. He has seen you and that is what matters. He is gathering His family around Him to witness His hand at work and to see His glory in action. I do not know exactly what all this involves for the moment but I believe it is true, for I carry in me the Spirit of His Truth, in order to give you the information that you need, in order to make an informed choice whether to believe Him or not. But you must surely ask yourself, What have I got to lose? Eternity is a long time for regret.

God, the Father, is speaking; He has come out of His rest for this final work.

Unto you that fear His name (aah, amazing; the name of the Lord's to value and respect in this context is 'the Lord of Hosts' (see verse 1), that name embodies His promise /assurance to us all: ie He is our LORD, and King, and defender and you are one of His and He will personally punish your persecutors) *Unto you that value His name, and the promise it holds, shall the* ***sun of righteousness*** *arise with healing in his wings; and you will grow up as calves of the stall.* This relates to the rebuilding and repairing of family and in this case He is talking about our extended heavenly family, including those who have already gone Home. We have been scattered and oppressed but when He comes, especially, we will all unite in love, as one with Them, in our real home. I trust and believe there will be a time of healing and refreshing in this life also for many of us.

'Good morning World!' Or I can confidently say it to those of you who are still listening - it *is* a good day! I have finally woken up (and I'm sure I can hear the heavenly hosts saying, It's about bloody time!)

The message for me today was simply given with some force, 'Get to grips with your shit and get on with the book and say, with confidence, Behold your God!'

Time to stop being a victim; I am a daughter of God and He is King, our Creator, lord of lords, King of kings; the very best of the best and He is talking to us. How incredible is that? How privileged are we? We have suffered, that is true, but He has seen and heard. Now it is time for us to wake up out of sleep, wake up to the truth, wake up and shake off the shackles of the earth and grab His outstretched hand and He will haul us up, out of the stink and the muck of this world that clings on and weighs us down.

I know that some of you are thinking that it isn't possible, that you have sunk too low; I have been to that dark terrible place... I know. But, nothing... *nothing* is impossible for God; our God. But we have to believe; we have to individually grab the message and own it, claim it as our own. Take that as your confidence. Know for certain that if you simply believe that you will be going to the best family reunion ever. You are cordially invited: the venue is a surprise and the exact date is yet to be announced, but you can be there. All you have to do is accept the invitation and be ready and all you need to put on/wear is belief in this truth and tart it up with a splash of eau de confidence... and then we will all be looking and smelling *sweeeet*! I love Him! No one can match the Lord, and our Father and the Holy Spirit (our family). How could I ever doubt Him? I would feel ashamed, except for the fact that He has said I must not feel ashamed, I've done what I could. This life can be a bastard. He understands. But there is hope; all is NOT lost; it's *NOT* a complete shambles! Hello people. It is good to be alive. I pray that you can or will feel this too. That is the work of the Spirit. Do your stuff Holy Spirit NOW - pleeeease! In the wise words of somebody, Praise the Lord! Praise our God!

PART TWO

No small print clause to manipulate you;
it's out of our hands:
This is our compensation.
Patience is the game we must play and we should be experts, we do it every day. (by me)

CHAPTER 9

January 1st 2011: The first Message was given on this day,

'Go to the lost sheep and say, Rejoice and be happy...

...*The Kingdom of Heaven is at hand*' (Matthew 10).

Freely I have been given, therefore freely I can give.

The word 'kingdom' can also be translated (from the Greek) as King, so this first message is the declaration that the coming of Our heavenly King (the Lord Jesus Christ) is fast approaching; very close indeed.

The Father's heavenly Kingdom, His and our final home, is a permanent place of happiness and power and it will continue forever. Jesus Himself declared to the Jews that the Kingdom of God was near during His time as a man on Earth, and if the Jews, as a unified nation had believed in Him, the Kingdom of God would have been established then, with Jesus as their ruler. He would have still had to die first on the cross but solely at the hands of the Romans, and then He would have returned in His glorified form to rule on Earth. This will still be fulfilled, after He has come to take us home. He will return to Earth, with His court officials, which includes some of His original disciples and He will be overall ruler of the Earth for 1,000 years. The people who remain on Earth during this time will have to become Jews and live under the Law, if they are to enjoy the benefits of His rule. Prior to this however, there will be a period of dreadful hardship and suffering for the Jews (and, I guess, for the other people who are left behind), and it will be more harrowing than anything that they have experienced in their history, which is hardly pleasant so far. People, who have rejected His call and scorned His invitation, will be crying out for God, pleading for Him to come and rescue them. (This is obviously a very brief explanation but it is nevertheless a warning for the Jews: search your Torah etc, all of this is prophesied!)

These terrible times of global unrest have started, in that certain events are beginning to unfold. The recent events in Syria are significant and connected to this and prophesied (in the Old Testament Book of Daniel and so on). The signs are very clear. There will also be an increase in natural disasters like earthquakes and suchlike; a decline in certain animal species and sea life is also prophesied. It's all in there. In fact this is evident to all at this time, but some will argue that historically there have always been natural disasters and political unrest and wars, what is happening now is not unusual. What is unusual is that the troubles won't improve this time around.

Another dictator is going to come to power, somewhere in the Middle East, in the not too distant future, and it will seem as if he has all the answers to the present financial problems.

I will be honest, so far I have not personally sought the Lord for any detailed information regarding the political and financial events relating to this dictator. I believe he is referred to as the Beast (Old Testament), who is simply another false prophet (he will unite with a spiritual leader, possibly the Pope or such like) and the man of sin and the Wicked (revealed by Paul in the New Testament) and there are other characters (eg the false prophet mentioned in the Book of Revelation !9:20) who feature in this also. Paul also explained that the wicked one (this particular dictator) will be destroyed by the brightness of the Lord's coming. I believe that Paul is speaking here about when the Lord comes back to rule here, not about His appearing in the clouds to take His followers (us) home but I might be mistaken. I am not claiming to be an expert in these particular things. I know as much as is necessary.

As believers we do not need to worry about the small print or understanding exactly what will happen after He appears in the clouds to lift us up and away from this troubled Earth, when only those who are looking for and waiting for Him will see Him come. However, if you are interested, purely as an exercise, please feel free to search the scriptures and seek or ask God for the answers yourselves, but I recommend that you don't get fanatical about it. Much learning is destructive. I prefer to focus on living for today and enjoy my relationship with Them. I am looking forward to some joy in this life and plenty in the next. The people who remain when we are gone will reap what they have sown and they will learn not to mock God that is for certain. He is very real, mark my words. He will rule and even then there will still be hope.

The limited knowledge I do have is sufficient to persuade or confirm to me that the end of this present time, the dispensation of grace, is coming to a close and the understanding and the messages I have been given relates primarily to the joyful coming of the Lord for those of us who can and do believe in the Son of God, Jesus our Lord and saviour, and those of you who have good hearts and who can believe that this invitation to join us is true. For us it is, and most defiantly will be, a time of massive celebration. This prospect does excite me. We are going to party...with Him, and drink the new wine at His table and it will be some celebration for sure.

The Lord intends to actually return to live on earth again after this and when He comes on this occasion the skies will open and He will appear for all to see riding on a white horse with several armies from heaven, who are also on horseback, and His name is Faithful and True and The Word of God (the sharp sword that comes out of His mouth are the words that He will speak, not a literal sword. It actually means an acid tongue that will cut to the core; He won't be messing about and talking sweet talk at this stage of events, this time He will mean business; He will indeed be listened to and obeyed by all) and He is King of Kings and Lord of Lords on Earth (see the vision and prophesy given to John in Revelation 19) for a thousand years. Even though this will no longer be the dispensation/time of grace, (which simply means something that is poured out) and during this time the grace (the acceptance and freedom and generosity of God) is there for everyone to enable us to come to the Him without any worries or fears and find help and hope and love and strength and forgiveness etc etc; even though when He rules on Earth is will be a more rigid rule, God is not a tyrant or a bully so there will still be grace and kindness for those who bow the knee to Him or acknowledge His authority and can grasp that He is there to help, during that time.

The fact that after the period of dreadful tribulation and suffering He is prepared to come to earth again shows His incredible grace and love and what a caring God He actually is, because even those who have rejected and ridiculed Him and His followers with venom will be given *another* opportunity to find some eternal or everlasting peace and reward and make it home, while He rules on earth. If they refuse and reject His authority at that time, then they are on their own. No more hope. Eternal pain and suffering waits for them. They deserve what is coming. C'est la vie, as the saying goes, you simply cannot help some people, but He is giving it a fucking good try.

The time of tribulation before He returns to earth will be like nothing ever seen, or experienced, previously in Earth's history. Satan will be vicious in the extreme because He will no longer have to pretend and lull anyone into a false sense of security, or bully others, in order to stop them believing. At some point previous to this Satan is restrained or put in prison and then released to vent his final fury. This will be evidence of anger and bitterness in extreme. During this time God will leave the rest of the world (who have rejected His Son and His love and the truth and His faithful prophets) and the arrogant Jews (who still cling to their Laws) will be left to get on with it, while everything spirals out of control. It is almost too terrifying to contemplate or think about. It makes me so thankful to know His grace; that I have the heart to hear and see; and the God given common sense to hear His call. Anyone who wants to dig their stubborn stupid heels in and stick around for the really tough times is welcome.

I now realise this is a warning, or advice rather, primarily for young people and those who are yet to be born. Those who have died so far still mocking God in their stubbornness and futility are going straight to hell. No more chances once you are dead. Those who have taken their final sleep believing in the truth, who have good hearts, will wake up in heaven. I know which I would choose. I trust I will be here when He comes in the clouds and we fly up to meet Him in the air; He has declared He is coming soon! Pretty please Lord. (I am knackered, fed up with all the pettiness; time to call it a day... it's a dayyyyyy! Knackered is an understatement, but I *am* happy occasionally, to be fair. I've got soul man, just not the musical variety for the minute.)

I will call it a day for today, but first I *must* stress that you have nothing to fear. We have *nothing* to fear if we can believe He has seen us, if we can hear His call. We will be out of here before the world truly descends into total chaos. Events of the final days are only just beginning to warm up and we will be long gone before the final dreadful events.

For you and us, the message is all good:

'*The glorious Kingdom of Heaven is at hand*' God bless, guys.

The second part of this first message (from Mark 2:1-12) *Your sins are forgiven,* relates (in context) to how readily we criticise others and judge others for their faults. We all have faults in our character and in the way we live our lives and do things, which others might view as immoral or weird or excessive. I cannot think of particular examples at this very minute; I am sick of it all. Sick of apologising for who I am; sick of hearing people verbally running me and others down and taking advantage. For years I have tried to conform to man's idea of what is socially and morally acceptable, tiptoeing around. If I relax and be myself I am wrong, if I keep quiet I am wrong, but more importantly it sticks in my throat when others feel they have a right to judge my faith, especially those who should be equipped to make righteous, or the right judgments. I cannot see how it could ever be right to succeed by trampling on others, who might be weaker or more vulnerable than ourselves. (It is good to vent your spleen; nothing wrong with that; we all have things that get on our nerves! That is different to deep seated troubles/worries/angst. I am uptight myself for a moment and the words I am searching for will not come; my creative flow is disturbed; I need to calm down and come back to this refreshed later. Aaaaaargh! Chill baby!)

Some might consider that I am equally guilty of criticising others for expressing themselves, and of course, they are at liberty to say what they like. I have been guilty of this in the past, I do admit this, and I am learning not to take what I hear said about me too much to heart and what is said about others at face value. My confidence is based on what I believe to be right according to God's opinion of me. I was prepared to 'conform' again to how others feel I should behave and I almost believed what they wrongly said about me, but He insisted again and again that I have done nothing to be ashamed of.

The danger with vicious verbal abuse (as oppose to pulling

someone's leg in fun) is the long-term damage that it can do and the distress it can cause to the individuals who are under fire or under scrutiny (it is just as damaging as physical abuse). This is what offends the Lord. And this is why we must let go because it is a vicious cycle. Until quite recently the accusations that I know are being made against me would have caused me to spiral down very quickly to the point where I want to kill myself and for a brief moment yesterday (30th August 12), as I was waiting to cross the road, I considered stepping in the path of a speeding car. It just flashed through my mind how easy it would be, and that scares me.

He decides what is acceptable and what is not acceptable behaviour and one of the greatest sins or faults in His sight is this arrogant tendency in some to imagine that they have a right to gossip and whisper lies about or be slanderous against *innocent* people (it is right up there with murder and lying, which we have already covered at length). The difference with arrogance (which is totally different to having confidence) is that it can often be a product of, or the consequence of, ingrained bitterness that has not been addressed or dealt with. (Clearly some characters are inherently arrogant and obnoxious, as I observed earlier.)

When the Lord talks about sin (faults) He is not criticising people for understandable little mistakes and carnal pleasures of the flesh (sex), or for the other things we enjoy. It is the wickedness in man's heart (in the form of bitterness and arrogance, premeditated murder, sexual abuse, vicious blatant lies that are designed to harm others, etc); these are offensive to Him. (Catholics have to go and 'confess their sins' to the priest. He said, *Your sins are forgiven you:* HE has the final say on this and this is His final say. Being forced to repeatedly confess can be a means of intimidation and is often a method of control by the leaders of Churches, keeping people down. In the Lord's time, He did advise some individuals to go and make an offering (under the rules or guidelines of the Law) and tell the priest what *He* had done for them by healing them or whatever. But it is no longer necessary to keep confessing every little thing we do or think or say, as we can go straight to God and tell Him anything we need to get off our chest, anything that is troubling us. He only rarely expects us to confess our mistakes to anyone else and explain the sordid details of things we have done. Speaking to a non judgmental professional therapist (about things that have happened to us that are destroying our lives) is a completely different matter. This unburdening is helpful, because it prevents the eternally destructive impulses from being acted out. I hope this makes sense. Most of us have baggage that is eating away at us. It is so incredibly sad the guilt and the burdens that many people carry in these modern times, and it grieves the Lord that others would take advantage of this.)

In the case of this particular man who was healed by Jesus, it seems the man had some cause for bitterness (because he was sick of being sick or whatever) in his heart and this is why the Lord said that his sins were forgiven. The Lord understood the man's reasons for being bitter; something was eating away at him, but He was expected to let it go. The man evidently wanted to be able to roll up his bed and walk away with it (see the reference) and the Lord said, in effect 'I have seen you; I have heard you. Take up your bed and walk and stop being angry about it.' The greater sin was actually in the scribes (v6, 7) who were watching and reasoning and making accusations in their hearts and criticising and condemning Jesus for His actions in releasing the man from the physical and psychological bondage that he was feeling. Bastards!

He is saying to you, to us now, exactly what He said to that man and to the Jewish scribes; He (Jesus) is God and He has the power, the authority to forgive anything, and when He forgives He also forgets. That is the end of the matter. Sadly, some people cannot see in their arrogance that they have done anything that requires forgiveness. They are not prepared to let go of their crap. Neither can they see that He forgets our mistakes. This forgiveness; knowing that He does not criticise or blame us for anything once we accept that He is true and acknowledge our weaknesses, is the greatest healer of damaged hearts. If we deliberately or consciously continue to make false accusations to hurt others following this forgiveness it is a tough road back from that place, if you have a conscience. It is not impossible but the next time it is the guilt and self criticism that can kill you, in extreme.

It has taken me a long time to grasp this, that He is so wonderfully forgiving of my mistakes (partly because others continue to criticise me, as I am attempting to let go of shit) so don't expect miracles, it might also take you time to get your head around this. But miracles most certainly do happen and I ask the Holy Spirit to do His bit so that in your case you get a miracle; the power/authority is in His word. Some of you who are listening now are looking for closure and have evidently been asking for forgiveness or assurance, or hope,.....

...therefore, hear and believe this message, whatever anyone else has to say,

Your sins ARE forgiven you.

1st September 2012: Before I continue with the messages I must bring you up to speed with my daily life. Yesterday I had a session with the counsellor and although I feel encouraged that I am making positive progress shedding all the poisonous baggage that has been dragging me down most severely, this morning I had to ask if I will ever feel excitement and enthusiasm for anything in this life, apart from this book (and my children and grand children), ever again. Despite the things I have written about fear, I myself am still weighed down heavily by the fear that my life will never change for the better, that I have been mistaken in my understanding of some of the promises that the Father has given me about the new life that is coming.

I wonder is it possible to miss oneself, in the same way that I miss my dad and both my sons and my friends? I do long to experience the joy of knowing that another day has begun. I regret that the events of my life have repeatedly knocked that sense of wonder and excitement of being alive, of wondering what the day will bring, of knowing that I am loved and safe. So, in that sense, I do miss me because the person I truly am is positive and happy and I hope that person has not been destroyed for the remainder of my time on earth. I know that isn't true because He gave me that joy and He doesn't take His gifts back. There are things yet to happen before I can truly be happy again; He's not lying.

As I type I recall that when I turned to the Bible app on my 'phone earlier and I was led to Isaiah 62, my 'phone froze up momentarily, my emotional temperature is decreasing but I'm reminded of the sign I was given, No Cold Zoning! Ha! OK, I get the message... again!

The message for me this morning from Isaiah 62 is that I will not rest until this book is complete and 'the righteousness that it contains goes forth as brightness and the victory and deliverance it declares as a lamp that burns'. I'd better get my arse in gear get this finished, be more proactive and start being more and more consistently positive about my faith in Him that's for sure, otherwise you will not see His brightness shining on the victory. Not through me anyway. And I won't get my break... eek!

There is also a promise of a new name for me, which His mouth will speak (this was something else that I was considering while slurping my coffee, what to call myself when my divorce is completed). The most encouraging thing about this particular message on this bright morn is that I will no longer be considered to be *Forsaken,* by myself or by others. These latest feelings of despair were provoked by criticisms/hurtful remarks made by close friends. I understand why they have made these remarks but their criticisms aren't based on what is actually happening in my life. I am hurt but there ya go! I'll live. This one won't scar me for life and the Lord will show them (and me) that they are wrong in their judgments about me, for His glory. Onwards and upwards! Tally ho and all that jazz. Why have I gone all posh and horsey?

The third part of the message (he he, I need to listen!) *Peace be unto you!*

John 20:19-21 Peace be unto me also: the Lord is saying to me '*even as My Father hath sent Me, even so send I you*'. This is pretty straightforward. These were Jesus' words to His disciples when He came back to show them that He wasn't dead but in fact, was very much alive and flourishing. This is about the size of it for you and me also. We can now be at peace because He has seen and heard and we will live with Him. We all strive for peace in ourselves, so this is a great gift. Praise the Lord, thank you Father. Thank you.

(World peace cannot be achieved until He returns to rule on earth. Be assured He will sort it. And he will restore the ecological balance and everything else while He's at it.)

I have already touched on the fourth and final part of the first message (12:34), when I advised that you must feel free to ask Him for answers yourselves, about anything that interests you or is a concern to you.

(Luke 10:9) *Unto you it is given to know the mysteries of the kingdom of God.* Understanding is given to all who ask for it. Information and understanding of that information is power. This is not an exclusive club, but I will remind you in advance to be aware that the Oppo will take an interest in you if you take an interest in understanding the Word. He might rock your boat or rattle your cage a bit, but it is just noises off stage; pay no attention, if you can. It will be worth it. Pass the message on to anyone you know who cannot read, because God does indeed speak in many ways to all, including children (although children are not expected to understand some things). Keep it simple is His enduring advice and a good motto. No stress required. God, I think I've finally got it!

If only I could see it, I have a very simple life but I yearn for some exciting rest (it's called a break or a holiday, I believe). I need to learn to trust the Boss, our Father, again. I yearn especially to trust Him absolutely again. I used to trust Him emphatically, in the same way that I believe His word (that sounds like a contradiction, doesn't it?) The thing is to some, and to me also, it looks as if He has forsaken me and that I have been mistaken in my beliefs. This Book (and the message and the outcome) is not only for your sake. Time will tell all. Time will convince all... time will convince me; I bloody hope so.

Hold your head up, look up; Peace to you; Our mistakes and faults are covered; He is coming!

He is finally answering the most commonly known and recited prayer, which is usually called the Lord's prayer but is actually *our* prayer; 'Our Father in heaven... thy Kingdom come!' Thanks, thanks and more thanks.

(Revelation 22:20, 21) He says, 'Surely I come quickly, ie without delay, soon, suddenly or by surprise, Amen or So be it'.

'Even so, Come, Lord Jesus'. Or, in the words of somebody, 'Make it so, Lord!' or perhaps it should be 'make it soon... please!'

The grace of our Lord Jesus Christ be with you all.

CHAPTER 10

4th September 2012: This morning I intended to tell you about the nail in the sure place, but the morning, for one thing, has taken a very uplifting and most unexpected turn, which I will tell you about in a minute, and the other thing is, the morning is no more; it's now way past midday (how much time do I have left to finish this?) I am in the process of editing and of course I've already said about the nail... perhaps I've got it wrong about my marbles!

This is the time of harvest in God's calendar, which briefly means that many *are* listening, hearing His call now in this brief window before the gathering storms begin in earnest (poor Earnest, indigestion is a pain in the gut). Seriously now, the winter is fast approaching for this world. But clearly there are those who are all ready and waiting to be gathered into His kingdom. If this makes little or no sense for now, no worries, I trust it will make more sense in due course.

However, sticking to the messages of the day for me, simply because I enjoy sharing these things with you, because I can and it is right to do so; I can be generous and share anything that might help or encourage. As I was saying yesterday, I rarely get excited by anything these days and I get depressed simply because people do talk a load of bollocks, sometimes.

But sometimes bollocks is good. Not everything we do or say has to mean anything (all is vanity!) but some people do go on and talk a load of tripe. Give me strength. Getting slightly off track here. Am I talking tripe?

I can never predict Him; He is generally unpredictable but consistently reliable and safe. There is no one quite like Him. We all share characteristics of His, but He is the sum total of everything. We could not contain His fullness in this mortal body and mind. It would drive us insane. Therefore do not stress or worry if you cannot grasp much. Simply take and enjoy what you can. We put too much pressure on ourselves and on others and this can cause us to burn out. We have to do what we can. The Lord said to His disciples, when they criticised a woman for 'wasting' expensive ointment a few days before the Cross. She rubbed the perfumed oils into Jesus' hair and cleaned His feet with it and the disciples, who evidently could not see what was coming as clearly as she could, were indignant. The Lord rebuked them for their criticism of her and said, 'let her alone, she has done what she could'. He recognised that it was her way of showing Him that she understood, to some extent, what was about to happen to Him (she was anointing His body for burial, according to custom) and more especially showing her great love for Him. The disciples were always worrying and squabbling among themselves (often about money or food) and not paying attention to the important issues, which He was talking to them about. On this occasion He told them straight, basically to shut the fuck up; time was short. He was about to endure His greatest suffering to date; He was due to leave them for a while and their lives would be thrown into chaos for a brief moment, until He returned with the new message of hope and peace etc. But they were still behaving like ignorant silly children. It's a good thing He knows how limited we are, but we could all make our lives so much easier if we would shut up and listen some times. Especially now, while He is speaking.

He has said I will have a new name and that I will have a place of my own to live and I won't have to move again (except for short trips/holidays, whatever) until He comes. That name is a surprise. Can't wait!

Following this extended version of the morning cogitations and chewing of the cud, it briefly crossed my mind that it's not a bad thing to be late because it seems to me that the Lord is usually late, by my standards anyway. It feels like He is late fulfilling one or two events that I am waiting for (I'm a grumpy bugger these days) and we've been waiting for Him to come and get us for over two thousand years. There were several other personal messages delivered firstly by the wren who has a monotone song, which grabs my attention most mornings; these tiny birds huddle together in the winter but he or she was whistling at me again this morning to get me to look up. (I'm crap at this! And He is so patient and loving.) Then, the word of the day in the dictionary - ramose, which means having many branches: His people are spread out in all directions. I cannot recall if I have mentioned this before, or even later, occasionally the Lord gives me a puzzle to do. He throws me a question and then gives me clues to pick up and piece together in order to get the answer. It keeps me distracted and lifts me out of the gloom that so easily settles around me

(which you haven't missed - I certainly won't miss it. The words are doing that thang again; I must be tired.)

Focus on the best bit from this morning woman!

On my way back from Welcome Break, I was accosted by an elderly gent who has since become my friend. He stopped me in my tracks and commented on how he had seen me regularly walking at great speed (actually I am generally sauntering and gathering momentum as I pass his house) most mornings. We exchanged a few pleasantries and then he asked what I do and I told him that I am writing a book, which is an autobiography that also shows the human side of the Lord, as well as His glorious personality. It was refreshing to know that I could openly tell him what I am writing about and get a completely positive response, which led to him opening up and explaining that he believes in the Lord and how he had experienced one or two unusual little things, including the hoot of an owl in the early hours of the morning, and that to him it felt as if someone was trying to tell him something, send him a message. He had mentioned it to one or two people who had laughed in his face, but my honesty had encouraged him to share it with me. I told him how the Lord regularly talks to me in this way and that it's a blessing (or words to that effect).

Later, when I initially sat down to type, I had to check out the meaning of the word owl in the Strong's Bible' concordance (you can get an android or an app for this; or in hard copy, of course... very useful), and then I had to run back around and tell the guy that owl means hold together and an angel. He misses his missus massively and I guess it will be a comfort to him to know that they are bound together forever and an angel (in the form of an owl) was calling out to him to let him know. I did emphasise that she is OK now and waiting to see him. It won't be long I suppose before they see one another again. What a rush, what a buzz! This is what excites me; seeing Him in action. I can be patient and wait my turn to share some real one to one time of blessing with Him.

When I talk to individuals about God and my experience, it makes me realise what a huge capacity I have for the truth. My appetite for the truth and the things relating of God and eternity and such like is endless, bottomless, my greatest joy, but I appreciate that not everyone can stomach these things in such large portions. I am constantly hungry for more of the truth; for more revelation of my eternal place. And I can see why I have to lighten this up a bit and fill in with chit-chat and so forth. Trust me there are truths that I am not ready to hear or understand yet. And I am ready for a break, I like others things too! There are things I chose to ignore or avoid or turn away from. I have to just hand those over to Him and trust He will deal with them, make them happen or whatever. And spiritual things are tiring for this mortal shell; some revelations can make us ill. Daniel and John and others knew all about that; on more than one occasion the prophet Daniel '*was sick certain days*' after being given a revelation and others suffered depression and bad dreams, as I already explained. It can kick you about a bit. In fact the Lord told me this morning that I have had another double kicking recently (and don't I know it!); He has seen, He's noticed. The point for you is the message is in Chapter 8 and basically that is all you actually need to grasp. Anything after that is gravy. Read the signs of the times and know that it is true (Matthew 16:3).

I would be lying if I said I wasn't lonely. I am often

desperately lonely. I thrive in company. We are designed to be His friends. When the Father first created His first Son He saw that He would be lonely and therefore He also made us, to be His friends. There are so many lonely peeps in this world. 'I can empathise but I am so tired with empathising, Lord. Be merciful to me, your servant, who also happens to be your daughter. You know I will see it through to the end, although it has clearly been touch and go at times, but I ask for the strength to complete this work in double quick time because I am running out of the umph to keep going for much longer. Where is my soul mate? Do I have a soul mate? You have said...'

Psalm 17 (from the Amplified Version with a few minor alterations/additions) is a better prayer in my opinion (and in my opinion, my opinion counts for diddley squat; I'm on a downer today, sorry guys); I'll share it because it says what He has said and what I want to say, and it confirms that King David understood how I feel, all those centuries ago (there is nothing new under the sun, ya know):

'Hear my right cause, O Lord; listen to my piercing and desperate cry! Give ear to my prayer or request that comes from truthful and kind lips. Let my vindication come from you! ...You have proved my heart; you have visited me in the night; you have tested me and have found no evil purpose in me...'; These are the words the Lord used to tell me how He feels about me, but I suppose I have to agree because despite my opinion about myself and the opinions of some of my 'friends' I have never set out to deliberately hurt anyone. 'I have purposed that my mouth shall not transgress...' Sometimes we all have to *do* things which seem wrong to other people or piss other people off and upset them, and this is especially true in respect of His will but for that I should not have to defend myself; He says we shouldn't. 'Shut up Nikki, this could get complicated'; I will continue to let Him speak. '... by *the words of your mouth* I have avoided the ways and path of the Destroyer' (the Enemy, the bastard!) 'My footsteps have stuck closely to your paths, to the tracks of the One who has gone before us; my feet have not slipped (a shelf fell on my foot recently and split the bone but no blood spilled; I have managed not to kill myself or anyone else yet, though I have been sorely tempted to do both). Each time I have been tempted, I have called on God, when the Destroyer has tried to destroy me or tempt me to destroy others with words. I know you will hear me; incline Your ear to me and hear my voice. Show your marvellous loving kindness... (Why am I sharing this with you, Reader? He is marvellous though, the most caring and gracious Lord)... You who save by Your right hand those who trust and take refuge in You from those who rise up against them. Keep and guard me, as you would the apple of your eye (we protect our eyes because they are precious); hide me in the shadow of your wings, from the wicked who spoil and oppress me (some of my 'friends' are sailing a bit close to the wind in the light of this), my deadly adversaries who surround me (Would they have said such hurtful things if they knew that it has made me want to kill myself?)... they are wrapped up in the comfort of their own prosperity and have very nearly shut up their hearts to pity; (hence the scripture used as my request, from the Book of Job, at the beginning of this book)... with their mouths they make exorbitant claims and proudly and arrogantly speak. They watch me and chip away at every step I take (the Lord is saying this so it has to be true, He has seen and heard); they have set their eyes to put me down' (how sad is that? I have simply done His will, which they claim to know and uphold; do they know His voice as well as they believe they do or, have they been listening some of the time to the whispers of the destroyer? It upsets the Lord when we judge and devour one another. We are all important, we all have a part. And so do you, dear readers).

I leave those who have opposed me to you Lord; do as you will but be gracious to them, as you have been to me. Let's face it, without Your grace we are all screwed. But because you are gracious we who hear are all saved from eternal misery. (Praise Them. I am incredibly happy to know this).

There are some who will feel the force of His anger and fury; those fools who crash on blindly in their' arrogance; I cannot pray for them). 'As for me, I will continue to behold Your face in rightness and justice (He will prove His word to be right in every respect, on every issue); *and* I shall be fully satisfied when I awake (one day it will be His face that I will see first thing when I wake up and not that of the enemy), to find myself beholding your form and having sweet communion with you.'

(5th September 2012) Praise you Father, praise you Lord! Praising Them is what I can do. Contrary to how it might appear I do have much to rejoice about and be thankful to God for. Unbelievably, this morning my heart is filled with overwhelming sadness because I cannot relax and be myself, as financially I have no status or control and I am reliant on others for somewhere to live. I cannot stop myself from feeling vulnerable and insecure. It is a vicious circle that I am trapped in. I feel selfish but this oppression is out of my control. It is time I learned finally to rise above it though.

I was considering the danger of prosperity. When we are blessed and prospering, either financially, in the flesh, or comfortable and at ease or in rest spiritually, it could be very easy to forget that others are still suffering, still battling with their own demons. I also need to clarify that it is the *love* of money that is the root of all evil, not money itself. Most arguments/disputes/wars are based on power struggles, which are controlled by how much money (and/or oil, in modern times) an individual or business or country possesses. Money can be the worst vanity; financial prosperity is very nice but it is not the answer because it cannot be trusted. If we love money and value money and financial security and status more than God or the rest of mankind, then there is going to be problems. He has given us *all things to enjoy,* there is nothing wrong with enjoying prosperity if you have it, God begrudges us nothing. If we see someone else in difficulty and it is in our power to help, if we want to share, then that is acceptable to God. But to fight and bicker and use one's place of prosperity financially or spiritually against someone else, who is not as fortunate is despicable and not acceptable; that's common sense. There is no joy or enjoyment in that, except for in a wicked heart. We should not judge one another but we can make righteous judgments based on what we know to be true. And these are righteous judgments; rightly dividing the word of truth.

I must add, for the sake of some that I know, that the teaching we had in the group that we have come out from, was sound, good teaching; the problems arose because the man who was put at the helm, used his power to feed his own desires and consequently desperately robbed and hurt others. We suffered abuse under the cover of respectability and spirituality. The Lord knows. This man and his followers will pay for their sins/wickedness.

Apart from rejoicing in Them, my purpose and focus has to be to complete this book, to get the message to you guys and then the Father will show me where I go from here. Praise Them. Praise Them.

Little Jenny Wren is calling me to huddle in close and look up. I can do that. I haven't completely lost it.

I am pressuring myself to stop smoking now. I do owe it to my lungs. I need to be able to breathe! I wonder if I *can* stop? The Lord himself has never made an issue about my smoking, so His lack of concern has prevented me from worrying about it. I also know it makes me smell. When I said this to the Lord He said that I smelled sweet to Him and my faith was what He sees. He is not shallow as some humans are. My smoking has been a cause of offence for some, who should have listened rather to what I have to say. Also I am vain enough not to want my teeth to fall out and this is what persuaded me to stop last time. This time it has to eventually be for the sake of my lungs, if I want to still be breathing when He comes.

I suppose we know within ourselves if we need to stop. Common sense tells us that our lungs cannot take such abuse indefinitely. There are the odd one or two people whose defences are able to resist the effects of smoking, but these are the minority. I do believe, however, that our individual destiny, healthwise, is written in our genes (following typing in this observation I heard on the news the same evening, that scientists now have a kind of map of the gene configurations and how they can be manipulated and read to determine which diseases etc, we are individually prone to. Breast cancer was one of the first diseases they made these types of connections with, I recall now).

Our lives are mapped out, even though we do make choices which can add to or detract from our quality of life. More importantly, our spiritual and eternal destiny is written in our minds and hearts and that is what we carry forward in to the next life, in to heaven, His Kingdom or the new Earth. Regarding the welfare of our physical bodies, we can definitely hold back the years in the short term but we cannot change anything indefinitely. Sometimes it comes down to whether we care enough about ourselves and to be honest, I haven't cared about or valued myself enough recently to stop smoking and smoking has been the one small thing that I could chose to do, come what may; sadly it has been a friend in the lonely hours. But, for me personally, the time to stop is approaching. I have had sufficient, thank you. I do want to be able to breathe freely again. I am convinced that this will tie in with the prosperity and time of rebuilding to come that He has promised. He values us, so we should value ourselves. No pressure from me or Him on you. Life can be tough; don't we know it!

6th September 2012: I did see His *likeness* smiling at me

from the dark darkness this morning, very early this morning. It wasn't Him but it was someone (perhaps an angel) very much like Him.

My walk to Welcome Break was a happy one and I was more aware of the deep well of happiness and peace and love and joy that is within me. I can accept that He is preventing me from reaching into these depths and claiming what is mine, in order to keep me focused on finishing this work. My only regret is that I can only share it in small measures, with a select few, for the foreseeable future. Except, by the time you are reading this all of you out there will know about it and I trust from today you and I will be witnesses to the good things of God and not only the suffering and grief.

The minor issue of today was the ongoing question of whether it is time for me to pack in smoking; sucking on the fire and puffing out the smoke (I have to determine to stay chilled and calm and confident, set an example). Is it time, or is it too early; am I jumping the gun? I need help to decide; 'I'm listening, Lord'. It's a tough one; it is my friend... or is it? a friend I feel I can depend on but which will also bite me in the bum eventually (no surprises there then!), which sounds pathetic but I know some of you will understand. I cannot shed or discard my eternal mates/friends who give me grief, but there will come a time when I must walk away from this particular pain of a friend (ciggies, that is). I originally typed in *disGUARD* and I think this is the correct spelling because deep down me and my actual friends do really care for one another and when we are not bickering and criticising and fighting, I know the closest of them would be there for me and

I would be there for them, when we really, really need help. But for now I have to keep my guard up, keep my armour on because the enemy knows which knobs to press and one or two of my friends are knob heads. And they possibly think the same of me. Love 'em though.

As I said though, 'I am listening, sorry Lord 'We all do this so don't mock, you critics... or is it cretins? None of us shut up and listen readily or often enough.

I glanced at the wall and there was a sign; a picture of a man running and the words Fire Exit and an arrow, pointing away from the services. Run away from the fire, or walk away from the smokes? I know there will come a time and I certainly hope that I can have peace long enough to end this now, but I am not holding my breath. Words are very clever, aren't they? How appropriate they can be. As you may appreciate, I am struggling, funnily enough it is not at the prospect of cutting out the smokes but to believe that peace will finally reign in my world. As I said, I won't hold my breath, Ha ha ha! Happy days... the very minute I had typed this in, one of my best friends chewed me off for something that I was definitely not responsible for. Aargh! Deep breath, gal; we can do this... 'we can, can't we Father?' Can I actually finish this book? I could terminate my life. I am clearly a pain in the neck to those closest to me. Or I could move to a far off land and become a hermit for the rest of the duration. Yeah, right! (His reply: Psalm 118:17 You will not die but live and declare the works of the Lord. Fairy snuff!)

Moving on, and getting back to *listening to the Lord* (there is no one quite like Them!) Turning again to God's Word, the

Bible, my most reliable guide: Hebrews 12:12,13 lift up the hands which hang down, and the feeble knees; and make straight paths for your feet, in case that which is lame (as I said, I broke a bone in my foot a few weeks ago, but this applies more to those of you who are spiritually lame/hindered or incapacitated) is turned from the Way... follow peace with all men, without which no man shall see the Lord'; the chapter continues to remind me of *the root of bitterness.* You are not come to the Mount that might not be touched, and that burned with fire (in Moses' day) nor unto blackness and darkness and tempest.' The Jews couldn't handle this experience under the Law; it was too rough. Moses said he feared and shook with fright. We are come to the city of the living God, the heavenly Jerusalem, and to the innumerable company of angels; to the assembling together of all His children, on Earth and in heaven; the spirits of good hearts made perfect and to God the judge of all. And to Jesus, the One who has made a bridge for us to enable us to come to God with no fear, to be His people, friends, children for ever. But see that you refuse not Him that speaks because He speaks from heaven, and His word is given to warn and advise and help. The judgments on those who have despised and mocked His word are also here and our God is great love (toward those who hear Him) but He is a consuming fire also.

For our sake and your sakes, our new friends and readers, I must compose myself and be calm and not let this in house bickering and unrest affect me. I am under no illusions - if, for any reason I did not finish this book, God will get this message of hope out to you some other way; in fact, part of it is blasting out of the radio, as I am typing (Tom Jones; I want to come Home). God is everywhere; speaking to us all, much of the time; am I listening? are *you* listening?

As Timothy the apostle said, (2 Timothy 4:7) I must finish our course (he actually said that he had finished his course, which sounds like we finish a course of antibiotics or something. I suppose doing His will is a bit like a course of antibiotics because it gets rid of the nasty infection of this world. Do you understand? I bloody hope so; I am typing myself in knots here, with all these words. Excuse me, my patience is wearing a bit thin. I must compose myself, darling! I 'gotta have faith ' (Wham!)

Timothy's following message (v8) brings me very nicely to the promises stored up in the next chapter; Praise the Lord! You can take the P if you like, or take the praise, but my praises of Him are genuine; far better than wallowing in misery and these praises bring eternal reward. Bargain. I apologise for my confrontational attitude; I am in self preservation mode, but it cannot be helpful to you, my friends.

CHAPTER 11

I intended to tell you more about 'the nail in the sure place' but it seems the Lord has organised things so that I tell you about the Crowns first. The nail *is* in the sure and secure place, so we don't need to think about that one now.

7th September 2012: Things are definitely looking up, or rather I am definitely looking up... and listening... as I *heard* from another of His *likeness*, my lovely beautiful friend and sister Babsi, who lives in Austria. I wish that my command of language was more comprehensive; I wish I had words powerful enough to convey the strength of feeling that I have for friends like Babsi and her son, because *lovely* and *amazing* really don't do justice to their incredible spirit. We only met briefly again, in this life, but we know where we have come from and where we are going to and His love truly is the tie that binds us and, as Babsi observed so wisely, words are not necessary between us. We know that we will see one another again... one day, perhaps not until He comes to take us Home. Wait and see; only He knows.

My greatest joy today is that I am certain now that I can and do trust our Father and the Lord and His Holy Spirit emphatically to do what is right for each and every one of us. There is a wonderful peace that comes from such knowledge, which is of more value than anything we can gain in this life. This world is still spinning but thankfully He has made a way for us to get off this ride eventually. Praise Him.

John 13:33 *These things are spoken unto you that in Him you also might have peace.*

The Eternal Crowns given to us as kings in the heavenly Kingdom:

Taken from my Journal; (dated 17th January 11) 2 Timothy 4:8 'Henceforth there is laid up for me a *Crown of Righteousness'* and this will be given to all those who love and look for His appearing (those on whom He shines). We have nothing in this life but in Him, as members of His family, we are wealthy kings.

The Crown of the Wise: Proverbs 14:24 'The crown of the wise is their riches' (this one is for you Babsi, Chrissie etc, all my extraordinary, exceptional sisters and brothers, friend(s)! I love you guys xx)

8th September 2012 – Sometimes there are no words between these extraordinary friends and me, but we have the tie that binds. There is always love, words spoken in days past by a wise man, Paul the apostle

(1 Corinthians 13) On behalf of the Wisest of all. Love is an extraordinary thing and a precious gift. His love is binding us all across the miles, throughout the centuries, around the world. There is no one-to-one, face-to-face, conversation between you and me, dear reader, but we are connected; we are bound together with Him for safe keeping. There are times when it will feel as if we are hanging on by a thread, but that thread is of the finest and strongest silk which can only be

broken if we harden our hearts to His love, receiving or giving love, by allowing ourselves to become riddled with selfish bitterness. Bitterness eats away at a good heart. The only hope that remains is that you will be snatched from the fire if there is a shred of goodness remaining; and maybe only He can see it but that is what ultimately counts. Love never fails; belief, hope, trust, all these sometimes fail us and they are all important things to have but the greatest of these is love; love is what He is; His love for us is exceptional and it will never fail us. The ability to genuinely and unconditionally love is *the* most God- like quality. Give His love a go, if you haven't already. Accept the love that is being extended to you. What have you got to lose? (Radio: Follow Me by Muse, 'Follow Me I will keep you safe from harm' He is with me, with us and evidently with the Muse guys.)

The sun is finally breaking through on this misty morning and The Son is finally breaking through the fog in my mind and helping me to understand the things that actually matter in this life and the next; the things I need to say. Praise the Father, praise the Son, thank you holy Spirit; thank you friends. Praise the FUN I typed in place of Son. Yep... we could all do with a bit of fun, fun is worth praising and there is fun to come with the Son. (I'm getting tired, if you hadn't noticed. Time to chill. Bfn)

Our *riches* are the gifts He has given in His manifold wisdom and grace: everlasting life and love and peace and joy and rejoicing in knowing God, our Father as He really is. This is a crown we can wear with pride and which we will see in its full glory and beauty when His beloved Son comes to take us home.

The Wisdom of God has many, many facets; it is manifold, multifarious (what a lovely word, another one I like is magnifical, from 1 Chronicles 22:5). A rarely discussed fact relating to the Father's will and plan for mankind is that He also made the world and the universe to teach heavenly beings and dignitaries about the love and wisdom of God. The other reason was to make new sons and daughters, and friends, for His first begotten Son, Jesus Christ, Christ Jesus. To our mind both these reasons seem unnecessary because we cannot imagine that there is anyone in heavenly places who does not know God, or why They would need to make friends. But I think the second one is self explanatory, isn't it?

Surely heaven is a place of perfect understanding of all things? The truth is that only God Himself has perfect understanding. He actually *is* the font of all knowledge regarding anything that truly matters, and heavenly beings are still learning, as we are; still getting to know Him, and surprisingly some heavenly beings will never get as close to Him as we can. They are not sons and daughters or friends of God; they will remain servants etc. This is why they were created/made; this is their purpose.

As for me, (Ephesians 3:7-21) (little, weak, old Nikki Rollinson: if my friends and I can follow Him and know His love, then so can you... but you don't have to do my job), 'I am made a minister of God, in order to write this book and declare the truth', and the necessary gift of grace or favour to do this work, and the strength to do it are essential, otherwise

I would have given up under the pressure, long ago, this is a particular calling; not because I am extra special but simply because this is the job that I have been given to do; 'grace given through the holy Spirit, His power, working effectively in me' despite it seeming as if I am cracking up, losing it, going mad or whatever; the fact of the matter is, I am still here, hanging on by that thin strong thread; typing, believing, hoping... loving Him, His will and His people. This is a work of the holy Spirit and no credit to my calibre but the reward will be credited to me, who am less than the least of saints, is this grace given, therefore, that I should preach among the people (of all races and nationalities) the unsearchable, bottomless well of riches of Christ (the anointed One): and to enlighten, illuminate and shed light on the real truth so that all can see what is the fellowship, companionship, friendship, communion of the mystery. So much of the truth has been shrouded in mystery for too long and the truth is God wants us to understand and enjoy knowing Him. When Paul himself wrote these words 'the beginning of the revelation of the mystery of God, who created all things after and with the help of His Son, Jesus Christ', was being revealed for the first time since the very beginning of time. During the period of time since Paul first announced it, God has been showing heavenly powers and principalities His great wisdom, through His interaction with, speaking to and working with, ordinary men and women (ie *His church*; He is within us, not in a building). Basically God is showing beings in heavenly dimensions *and* we mortals (who are/will be immortal), that He is all powerful and that there is nothing He cannot do, or doesn't know (ie the manifold/plentiful and abundant wisdom of God), in the way He does things; even when His will is viciously and relentlessly opposed. (In my excitement I am doing my best to say this in the simplest of ways, so that everyone can understand.) 'This is the eternal, everlasting purpose, which He purposed in Christ Jesus our Lord' (our boss, friend, master, messiah etc). This began with the first coming of Jesus, the anointed one. (Take small bites of this, any of this if you're struggling to grasp it, because it is a lot to swallow in one go even with the help of the Spirit.)

It is in knowing the Lord, as He really is, through His faith in God, His and our Father that we can come to God with boldness and confidence. He has paved the way, as you have seen. Consequently, we desire that you faint not; don't give up, He has allowed us to suffer and for this we will be rewarded. There are many prayers going out on our behalf to our Father, and He hears because we are His family. Be strong and let the Lord live in your heart; believe it! So that, being rooted and grounded and established in love, we might understand, with all the believers in God, everything that there is to know about the truth and about His love and ... everything good. I ask that you might understand through these words, empowered by the holy Spirit, that you might know just how much He loves us, so that we can all be filled with the fullness of God; He wants to share with us as much as we can accept. He is not setting a limit but neither is He pressing or pushing us to take more than we want or can take in or grasp.

'Now... unto Him that is able to do exceeding abundantly above all we ask or think, according to the power, the force, the ability that is working in us, whether we can see it or not;

unto Him be glory and praise and rejoicing in us (His living church, His body of men and women) by Christ Jesus, throughout every single age group, throughout the generations, throughout time, world without end'; these praises will ring out for ever, in the new world that will never end. So be it.

There are more crowns to be gained but it is not necessary for me to list them all; you will all be given your own particular crowns, in due course. More praise to Him!

We shall be a crown of glory in the hand of the Lord, no more called or feeling forsaken, as He delights in us. He has set other Watchmen to guard and protect us and who pray for us continually, to keep us safe from being lost eternally. We should unite in our hearts, in these last days, and ask Him to fulfil everything, and give God no rest, until He comes.

CHAPTER 12

9th September 2012 (19 minutes past 6 pm): It has taken one mother of a headache and several hours' sleep to find the words to type today. The pain in my head began to emerge on Friday evening and was ironically slightly alleviated by a hoofing Led Zeppelin tribute concert (by Hats off to Led Zeppelin; thanks guys, fucking brilliant by the way!) I am like Him because I am not predictable.

Last night the pain started to get worse so I went to bed early *(He gives His beloved sleep!)* I had a nightmare and I don't usually have bad dreams (my friends have bad dreams but I am generally saved from this particular curse, so it caught me out). All my pent up anger was poured out, as I trashed everything in sight (details are fuzzy now, thankfully). When I woke up I recalled that the Lord ransacked the Temple in Jerusalem in a rage against the leaders and the money changers. I cannot physically do this, it's not necessary, but I am also angry with the leaders in some of the modern day churches; I am angry with the people who are supposedly representing the truth and God, one of whom has nearly destroyed my own life and the lives of my friends. I am angry too because I am/*we* are, still feeling the repercussions of that and, speaking for myself, I am still battling to regain my full faith and peace and confidence in Him.

I had to ask myself again this morning, 'How can I speak to you, my friends, with conviction and tell you that everything will be alright, when I cannot see it myself?' I still have days when I cannot see Him, when I feel forgotten, in spite of all the daily assurance He gives. It feels like all words and no action.

I cannot accept that I am asking again, 'What is the point of my life, Lord? I might as well be dead as no one needs me here.' My head was thumping and I felt as if this world is poisoning me. I needed an answer to that question in order to continue writing to you.

The answer finally came eloquently through the Word and also while I was reading a book called Cherry by an American ex-hippie chick called Mary Karr: (I have had to extract quotations from her book for your benefit, but with slight changes, I trust she understands). (October 29th: These quotations appear to have disappeared and I've passed the book on. Hopefully her observations will come back to me. Fortunately I remembered, or was reminded, that I sent these quotes to my daughter Chris via text...phew!)

(I quote) 'We are in a place where all the love has been sucked out of people, but the husks of them kept staggering around and trying to take stuff in. I am myself. I am here solely for embellishment and witness. I am here to watch.'

I myself am here and I must stay to finish what He has started. Following this I added, for Chrissie's sake, 'Of course we are here to do more than watch; we have a work to do. He is coming and we have nothing to fear from Him. In the world we will have troubles but be of good cheer, He has overcome the world and prepared a better home, a wonderful home, where we will live forever as kings. Praise Them. The headache was worth it!' Have to also add to this text that it was evidently right that my original typing was lost because hopefully you have benefited from this additional encouragement...and so have I.

!0th September 2012: (Why did I think it was the 10th of December?) Last night I was in too much pain to continue typing but I now have the combination of drugs sufficiently balanced to enable me to be upright. I trust I will be OK in a day or so. During my usual morning' constitutional earlier I met a guy who sows all his treasures onto his hat. My treasures and my pain are sown into this book, along with the Lord's. It is at times like this that I realise how wealthy and blessed and privileged I am. It is my duty but also my pleasure therefore to speak with you. I have no idea how some of you will get to hear the great news but that is a job for the Holy Spirit.

It is very painful believing that no one would miss me if I wasn't around. It is painful and sad to have no one to turn to during the dark hours of the night, when our heads are full of doubts and fears. I understand. The fact is He cares; He has seen; God *is* listening and watching. He is here. (11th Sept, I wanted to write December again! This morning I met 32-year-old Dean, from the Forest of Dean, a Big Issue seller, one of the seemingly *forgotten ones*, who are sleeping on the streets. You made my day, mate. You represent the very people He is calling in and reaching out to. Even if, for some reason Dean, you cannot read this, you have the message that our Lord is coming to take us home. You have seen His hand working in your life, as you explained, in a way that you understood. Hopefully you now understand even more that it is most certainly Him, our Saviour, Christ Jesus, who is with you in your beleaguered, humbled circumstances. Evidently Dean was living on the street, selling the *Big Issue* magazine, not because he had been affected by a combination of issues, as in family or childhood problems or illness or loss of loved ones or financial ruin on a large scale or drug or drink additions, that had caused him to have severe psychological problems, thankfully. My reason for assuming this was that he did not appear to be overly troubled, and even though he was on the street he did not feel sorry for himself and could even rationalise that there were people who were much more worse off or hindered than him! He was hardly affected by the obvious prejudice against him, particularly from the immigrants whom he was defending. I have to believe from the good I could see in Dean that he was not one of life's great actors. I trust him, my spirit witnessed to his spirit; he was also genuinely excited at the prospect of the news that the Lord is coming to take us home. He definitely knew of Him and knew His voice and word.

It is so much harder, I believe, when we have known comfort and good wages, to cope when our circumstances are changed dramatically by such issues (even relatively minor problems can appear to be too hard to endure). It is when we are attacked by a combination of problems that the smallest thing can push us over the edge, no matter how strong we believe we are. I know, as I have already explained, that without the Lord's hand on me I would have fallen into oblivion, I would be utterly lost. Dean is a year older than my son and a year younger than the one who was lost. The one big issue for Dean was losing the place where he was living because he could not pay the rent. I wonder, Dean, if you got your tooth fixed? Will I see you again in this life? I hope I do. Watch this space!...several weeks later, there was his smiling face, tooth fixed, waiting for my book. I have to pull my finger out and get cracking with it... finish it, that is.

The other answer to my question, 'What's the point of my existence?' came from Psalm 79; the message is that those who deserve to suffer will be suffering soon, they will pay for their mistakes. This might sound a bit blunt and a bit harsh, but there are some cruel, thoroughly wicked people (arseholes) who think they are untouchable, who mock God and hurt His people/the good people in this world. These bastards (and I have already discussed the types we are talking about) should be afraid, they should be very afraid. They have pushed His grace too far. There is still time for them to apologise but I doubt if they will be listening. On the other hand, those of us who have endured hardship, which is not self inflicted, or unfairly, have taken it for long enough. He has seen, He has heard.

(From Mary Karr's book) 'Be strong, help is on the way!... one instant you feel yourself spiralling into darkness and next the light streams down on a whole new stage set.' This world appears to be a stage set much of the time. We are all actors here, even those of you who think you are individual and straight up. We all assume a persona at one time or another to fit in or get through the day. That is just the way it is for many of us. We simply have to make it through another day, any way we can. We don't put on an act all of the time, although some do. I feel sad for them.

Mary (Karr) eventually found her own mantra towards the end of her book, her own pearl of wisdom and comfort: the simple words from the movie The Wizard of Oz *there's no place like home*. How true and appropriate this is. There is indeed no place like home. Some people are fortunate enough to make a semblance of home on this earth, a place of their own where they feel safe and warm and secure and reasonably happy. But others, like me, and Dean, don't have this particular, indulgent luxury, although I did have it for a brief time, praise Him. This is why it is comforting to know that we have a home prepared for us, in heaven. In fact I know I have a palace and a little villa. I have seen my villa; a wonderful brief vision of my perfect home. There was no doubting that it was real; I was there - I could see and feel and smell and hear everything. It is real. It is real. A friend called Annie might be interested to know that the light is amazing there and it has an amber glow. It is incredible. The air is warm and balmy and I could hear the children laughing and playing in the streets, somewhere in the distance. It was/is a place of pure bliss.

11th Sept. 2012: Please do not imagine for one moment that I am not thankful for the room and the bed and the food... and the love that my friend has given me, for a time.

Another writer, François Bizot, observed in his book *The Gate*, after he was released from a prison camp and he refused/turned down cold soup in a very posh house (I have had to alter the quote slightly to keep it brief but retain the meaning), 'a man who has endured hardship becomes an exacting and extremely sophisticated creature, little inclined to squander his essential skills or limit his capacity to find perfect happiness; he becomes persistent in his yearning for a real quality of life.' I agree, we are basically no longer prepared to accept second best (no insult intended for the provision made by my friends). For a short while, I have been forced to accept second best, ie not my ideal choice, but in Eternity God will give me only the best. Francois' words are so true, and to those who try to help us it can sometimes appears that we are ungrateful. I must emphasise that I am extremely thankful to my friends (and the Lord, who has orchestrated this) because I am now, in my own humbled circumstances, able to get this work done and out there, (and I am not on the street) thanks to their wonderful and timely generosity.

This particular morning I am happy because I see him much more clearly. I am booting out the echo of the demons that tried to destroy me. I remember why I am here.

Returning to 10th Sept. and still wondering what is the significance of the 10th of December:

I am here to give a message and say that He is true, He/God is real, and He is coming soon to take us home; *help is on the way!* We have nothing to fear and we can be at peace with Him, under His shadow. In the world we will have tribulation and trouble, but be of good cheer He has overcome the world and death, and has prepared another world, a better place, a wonderful home, where will live as kings and princes forever.

I appreciated the inclusion of the word 'stuff' in Mary Karr's Cherry ('people are trying to take in *stuff*') because a very good friend of mine uses this word a lot when he talks about what the Lord says to him, he gets *stuff* from the Lord. There are those who might question where I get my *stuff* from the Lord from but I really do not care because I know this *stuff* is sound and these messages truly are from Him, my greatest Friend(s) and Comforter. He can speak to me any way He likes!

My other question was, 'How much more of this oppression can I take?' I know the answer to this one; as long as it takes, as long as necessary ....I hope it's not too much longer, Lord. You can, and no doubt will, surprise us, as invariably you do.

<u>Kindness from you</u>:

Too long I tell you, too long I've spent, sitting here sweetly on the fence; Not wanting to offend... not afraid, just caring,

but misjudged at each step.

Don't take me for a fool, you who assume superiority and seniority;

I have been calm, I have been kind...thus far.

But fuck with me, now and treat me like your whore and I'll show you the force of my ammunition. Once again I will fight for my freedom, my say, and a little respect... I am not a game for men!

Friends are not friends when they use you to feel they are something, exposing they are not real. People like these will have you on your knees begging for bread, when they have left you for dead.

But do not be deceived, I know I am worthy; I know I am strong

(by Chrissie)

CHAPTER 13

I have a pressing issue to explore in this chapter.

Earlier I commented that I'm now finally dealing with the 'echo of the demons' that have tormented me and attempted to destroy me during the previous year or more especially. Whether this is simply a form or level of temporary mental illness or it is inspired by demons or a combination of the two, is hard to tell, without the help of the holy Spirit. 'We all have our own demons to deal with' is a term that most people are familiar with, but the involvement of actual demons is rare.

(18th September 2012 – I had to insert the following comments after I completed this chapter because they will help you to understand how I have understood this subject, in relation to my own life experience.)

As I have already said, during the course of the time it has taken me to type this book I have been seeing a counsellor and she has been instrumental in helping me to unburden and let go of my grief and anger relating to all the distressing things that I have had to live through, which, until a few months ago, I had rationalised and dealt with unemotionally. The rot started when close friends started to criticise and undermine my faith and conviction and confidence (as you know, but their questioning has strengthened my faith) and then the final straw came when I was applying for work and I was made to feel like I was swinging the lead (not trying), when they did not know my circumstances or background.

My reasons for bringing this up again is to explain that even knowing the Lord things take time to be resolved. This is not a quick fix; at present I do not have the power to heal on the spot, or cast out demons (if I did I would certainly have tried it out on myself and I would wear myself out helping others); I have known what it is to experience physical and mental illness and I also know without Him I would be dead. The next part of this is that having dispelled the anger and grief, I now am getting very panicky because I am afraid that I will be criticised, by new friends, and that the cycle will begin again if I relax and be myself (fears, which I have to add are unfounded so far). I feel I will be too much to handle; overpowering; too confident etc. I have no idea how to socialise without putting on pretence and dumbing myself down, to be honest. When I do 'contain' myself... I withdraw into myself and feel as if I am dying. When I am myself, I am not mediocre, run of the mill, inoffensive, one colour, bland; I am neither quiet nor reserved by choice, except when my hormones are raging; I am none of these things. I am not outgoing to draw attention to myself, I am outgoing when I forget about this shitty life; when I am me, I am simply happy and full of life 'full of the joys of spring' whatever my circumstances. I am simply me.

God Himself speaks of Himself in much the same way (the holy Spirit has just reminded me)... 'I am what I am (Exodus 3:14) I simply Am', in other words

'I exist, I am here'; He is here, 'He is Alpha and Omega; He is the first and the last, the beginning and the end'; everything we need is contained in Him. I too have something to give; I have a message of assurance and confidence in Him to share; I have joy and peace in abundance to share (when others are not attempting to restrain or control me). I have understanding about God and His ways and the way He thinks and acts. He does not conform but neither will He offend His babes (and by that I mean those believers who do not know Him well. Strong meat/teaching is only for those with maturity). He is amazing. There is no one just quite like Him. We all have characteristics of God in us, we all share a 'likeness', but He is extra special; Christ Jesus is extra special.

What was *the* point I knew I needed to tell you today? It will come back to me. This temporary memory loss is due to the fact that I am finally starting to forget the pain and the crap of the past (which I could so easily and stupidly hold on to, as I discovered one morning... as you have heard). Sorry guys. It really is time to move on: 'Onwards and upwards', as the jolly saying goes. I do have to focus one more time on the Enemy (this is strong meat/teaching)... just one more time. I am delaying doing this and trying to avoid it.

As I was drifting in and out of sleep this morning (12th Sept 2012) I was considering my new friend Dean and his circumstances (which appear to be fairly straight forward, although not ideal). More especially I was considering the continual battle that I have been fighting to hold on to my own sanity and also considering those poor souls who are afflicted or tormented by Tourette's syndrome (and other similar afflictions): what is that all about? It seems so unfair and cruel. Could this somehow be influenced by actual demons or is it merely a psychological blockage or affliction?

My attention was drawn to this because I was watching a TV prog last night and it explained that when people with Tourette's sing or play instruments their 'tics', I believe they are called, go away. Sometimes they can also control the effects in other ways, but the musical influence appears to be fairly universal.

There is an historical example of something similar in the Old Testament of the Bible, relating to one of the kings of Israel, a guy called Saul, which I will share in the hopes that I can find a satisfactory answer. Demons or devils or Satan's minions definitely do involve themselves, uninvited, in the lives of some extraordinary or random people, and it is prophesied that demons (the fallen sons/angels) will be more prevalent or conspicuous in the Last days.

This is not an easy subject to examine and discuss, mainly because I do not wish to scare anyone or give the wrong impression. Demon possession is over glamorised not only by the film industry (and TV programs) but also by the Catholic Church establishment and the High Church of England in particular, who encourage elaborate rituals, such as exorcism. These things/beings need to be understood and considered and dealt with properly and they do make a lot of noise and commotion (and can cause people to damage/cut themselves and hate themselves) but ultimately they cannot stand against the truth and His authority and His people. We are covered by His blood, His sacrifice. What I mean is, they are not more powerful than God and if you can believe in God they, and the problems they inflict, can be eradicated permanently. They are vicious bitter bastards, as I explained in an earlier chapter, and I am persuaded that they do torment innocent people who are vulnerable (which is why these things very often start in vulnerable childhood or early teens and affect bright or sensitive individuals). They simply get into their heads. I now understand that the leader of the cult used to talk a lot about the Opposition and the Enemy and gave him far too much time and he got in to our susceptible, often innocent, heads. I have to talk to you about these things because movies and books and TV do advertise the enemy/Satan in the wrong light, too often in modern times. He is not friendly or glamorous, neither is anything associated with the darkness he instigates or the nonsense he encourages people to believe as an alternative to the truth and the Light. Although I suppose stories of ghosts and witches have gone around for centuries. Give him an inch and he will take a mile, so I will try to keep this brief but take the opportunity to expose him further for what he really is.

Savants, who are also vulnerable, and child geniuses (for example, Mozart, Beethoven, even Jim Morrison, Kurt Cobain and other more recent musicians and composers); these poor people are driven to death by their talent, which Satan exploits. He gets in their head and torments them, drives them to madness and death, and destroys the beauty.

He infuriates me, because he also is here, walking around God's Earth. But, my eyes are fixed on the Lord and the truth and the truth will set them free, will set me and you free, if you can hear and believe. Praise God. Praise our Lord and Saviour.

The Lord's way of dealing with demons is not to be elaborate and dramatic. His way is very simple; basically all you need to do is ask Him to take these afflictions away, believing that He is true and real and that He hears and cares for you and, while the trouble and anguish Satan and his workers can inflict can be vicious and degrading in extreme, it does *not* involve spinning heads and spewing out green slime.

I need to explain that there are occasions where demons are not involved. Sometimes some sad people do act these things out to draw attention to themselves and this would be obvious to anyone who has had any prolonged experience or association with Tourette's (30,000 people are affected in this country alone, I have to look at this!) the same as with any mental condition or affliction. Of course, some diseases of the mind are genetic and can also be caused by narcotics or other external influences (as you will possibly already appreciate to some degree). This is a sensitive subject and I will deal with it as sensitively as possible, be assured.

Nevertheless, I am persuaded, looking at the relevant examples in the Bible, which spring to mind, that some of the more cruel afflictions *are* Satan's handiwork, inspired and used by him. I will do my best to get to the bottom of this. We already know the only definitive and long lasting solution, but I/we do need to understand as much as we can about these conditions/afflictions/disease(s) (un-ease, as in unrest or not in peace) from a scriptural viewpoint, from the Lord's angle.

Demon possession, when people have invited them in is rare. Sometimes, only occasionally we hope, people do have sex with demons. If you are fortunate enough to be reading this and you have gone down this route you most certainly will have regretted it or very soon will, the only way out is to ask the Lord to tell them to leave. This is not to be treated light heartedly. They literally are insatiable and have no respect for humans. I must emphasise this!

The Lord told me that in the past that the Holy Spirit has protected me from attack, otherwise Satan would have used any means he could to destroy me. They have sniffed around me and if you resist they are vile in extreme. But I must emphasise... this is, I would assume quite rare. We are covered by the blood of the lamb (His sacrifice protects us) and all we need to say is 'I am covered by the blood of the Lamb' if you ever feel they are trying to scare you. The Lord told me that Satan asked if he could be let loose to have a go at me, to show that he could turn me against the Lord (illness, loss, humiliation, degradation etc). The Lord permitted this for a particular purpose, as in the case of a guy called Job in the Old Testament days (see the Book of Job in Bible for details) and Satan tried to tempt the LORD Jesus, of course; and there is one other extreme case that particularly comes to mind from the time when Jesus, the Lord, was on earth. (I have to take a break from the laptop so I'll revert to a hard copy of the Bible and take a closer look at this subject and get some clear light on it, before I continue.)

What I will say, before I close down for now, is that the reason I have not had closure on my own afflictions is that Satan has been permitted to continue testing my faith to the extreme (this began with the abuse and deception by the cult leader and progressed to the ME, which is now healed and gone for good He has said; the Oppo' took my son, and my marriage, and my innocence and very nearly my sanity. He is still trying, but the Lord will heal me fully on every count, all this will stop when Satan is let loose to do His worst on the arrogant, wicked human bullies, who have deliberately attempted to destroy many, many lives around the world for centuries and, in some cases, have succeeded. In due time the Lord will deal with Satan and His 'angels' and they will be thrown into a bottomless pit, and they will fall utterly alone and in pain and torment for all eternity.

There will be a short time when they will be restrained in chains prior to this, hopefully before the Lord Jesus Christ takes us home (I will try to confirm this, check it out); some relief is imminent and I trust this book will enable everyone some immediate relief and respite to make a clear choice to believe Him and know that all hope is not lost. I am not certain at this time, exactly how this will work, but work it will, with the help and support of the holy Spirit, whatever happens. I must emphasise that the Lord, God is not making any demands on anyone to stop being themselves. This is ultimately intended to improve your lot; give you hope; peace, whatever you need.

Satan and his minions will eventually be released again to torment, and to cause havoc and extraordinary suffering on those who have refused, in their arrogance, to respect the Lord, and shown no respect for certain people who they have singled out to bully and torment, after He has taken us home. I must emphasise that none of this suffering and distress was ever

God's intention; it is not His doing or His desire. People, as do heavenly beings, have free will. We all have the right to choose what we believe and what we will do. However, no one surely chooses to be afflicted with Tourette's or similar mental problems or severe illness, these things are out of our control. Satan loves no-one. He only loves himself. (I have not finished exposing him; there is more understanding to come. The answers are here.)

13th September 2012: I met my friend Spider's son this morning. We have passed on the road a few times and nodded (as you do), but finally I was able to introduce myself. He too uses the early morning walks to get his head in gear for the day. I also met a guy called Elijah and it was refreshing to hear this fine name; unusual in modern times, except for in some areas in USA/America (or is that Alcoholics Anonymous? Another harrowing disease driven by the enemy).

I am encouraged when I find I can easily chat to strangers as if they are friends, it shows me that I am capable and approachable; I am not entirely alone. It invariably surprises me when people say they like me. I feel I am 'different'; I am different because I don't belong anywhere here; I have no permanent home. And I have strong views, which I tend not to air very often anymore; it's easier, and perhaps a tad cowardly, or maybe kinder to keep quiet.

I am also different because although I do adapt to a certain degree to fit in with the people I am with, I am never entirely relaxed and comfortable because I have become conditioned to expect them to dislike me (because I have been bullied and controlled in the past) and it possibly makes people nervous and consequently *they* cannot relax. At heart I am non conformist in this world, I struggle to conform. I am myself, but I must avoid causing unnecessary offence in less open minded company (among babes). There is too much prejudice in this world, fuelled by ignorance and old wives tales and ingrained beliefs and fears.

It is an effort for me to conform to other people's ideals of what is acceptable conduct to fit in to society, in much the same way as it is for a person with Tourette's to control their ticks, in order to feel 'normal' and accepted even if it is just for a short time.

I don't want to conform; some narrow minded people need to stop being fearful and elitist and prejudiced (I steer well clear of deceiving, cruel robbers/thieves and murderers with no conscience; the Lord will deal with them).

We are blessed with warm September sun and while taking a break (heavy stuff this, I need a break) to sit a while and soak in its rays, smoking a ciggie which I didn't actually need, I glanced over at the table outside, which was beautifully decorated with the early morning rain. It is easy to forget the pleasure to be found in the simplest things, which our God given senses can enjoy. As I swept the water away I relished the luxurious sensation of this pure, warm liquid running through my fingers, and understood and remembered why innocent children and individuals with autism and so forth, gain huge comfort and relief from such basic stimulation. For that brief moment I knew I was alive; I could feel; I was at peace, lost in the pleasure, touching God, in a sense, with my senses. For that one brief time all was well with the world, my crazy world. Even in this life, as an adult who has seen too much pain and disappointment and misunderstanding and rejection and abuse (but nowhere near as much as some poor people, by comparison to some I have only had a taste. It has been terrible for me, it's all relative). I know I am blessed and rich because I have not been so poisoned and tainted by these things that I cannot still feel Him, using the senses He gave us, in the simple (yet incredibly complex) things. His creation is complex: I do not understand how He made water and the light and every astonishing part of His wonderful, incredible Creation. Scientists might have the formulas but they do not have the power or the means to make most of these things easily. We have the mind of God, therefore the information and ability to reason or find these things out is innate in some men and women (inborn, established in the womb or from birth). This intelligence, understanding is also God given, we are programmed by Him. This is the truth of the matter, of all matter. My rabbit (not the other pleasure aiding 'rabbit') in the peanut is most defiantly nailed down in a safe place, which is one thing that matters a great deal to me; I hope I have explained about the rabbit in the peanut, representing my hidden joy. Split open a peanut and take a look. Are you still young and open minded enough to see the hidden joy? Use a magnifier if necessary. At the base of one half of the nut is the shape of a tiny rabbit. This is not a test that you have to pass, it is my sign; it is His way of showing me, of reminding me that my joy is still there, even if sometimes it is hard to see;. The question is, are you open minded enough to see. or are you so set in your ways that you cannot see His joy, which He has stored up for you?

As far as I can determine, the only real sin is in not respecting God and, by extension, other people. Respect for God is the beginning of wisdom. Those people who reject Him and deny His existence should be afraid because He has the power to throw them into Hell for all eternity. (Am I in trouble for politically incorrectly speaking? Do we not have freedom of speech?) I was thrown into the world and at times it has felt like a living hell but I have only tasted hell. I experienced briefly the utter, terrifying loneliness of it; the pain and frustration and the suffocating darkness, which you can feel. We are not invincible, neither is this life the end, it is the beginning. For some it is the beginning of a most amazing adventure; the prerequisite, the introduction, the place where we decide who we are going to believe and where we are going to spend eternity. The only real choice we make is between life and death and it is our heart and soul which determines this. We are all (who can read this) mature enough to make choices and this is a choice worth taking the time to consider. (Children and the simple souls and other innocents and even the uneducated in some cases go straight to be with Him. They cannot choose.)

The Bible is a guide, a way that God can communicate with mankind, as is this book to a lesser degree. It is not essential to be able to read to have a good heart, and this is what God sees. Goodness is either there or it isn't.

There are some uncomplicated souls for whom there is never any question. Their hearts are good through and through, right to the very core; there's 'not a bad bone in 'em'. But, looks can be deceiving and only He knows for sure. Some of us are given the ability to discern and at other times we are blinded to the true intentions of others, as myself and my friends were for many years. And sometimes He still hides the true character of some people from me. This is their opportunity to be honest with God; to face up to their fears and their reasons for rejecting Him. Some of the hidden characters are the ones who are self serving, men pleasers. Those of you whom I have known; you know who you are... and so does He, of this you can be certain. Can you change your mind in the time that remains? The clock is ticking and time is running out. This is not a threat; it is a fact.

However, getting back to devils, who were sons of God but they now have no shred of good remaining in them, they are bitter to the core. There are some people who are like this also and when they are punished, when they get it in the neck, they will get everything they deserve. And they cannot plead ignorance or claim He hasn't given them a chance. When they stand before Him He will say 'I never knew you and you never knew Me'.

Moving on (I'm slow to get off the mark today, 14th September 12), let's take a look at some examples in the Bible of those who were tormented by devils.

Quick break; the sun is out and the shadow of Jenny Wren fired me to look up to the good things and away from the gloom that has been hanging over me so far today.

I can do this; here goes! Time to get some more answers about unclean spirits or devils.

The first example that I feel inclined to examine from Matthew 12, actually ties in with my previous observations concerning good and bad souls or spirits (celestial or terrestrial or heavenly or earthly). (I just twigged; Peter, by the wisdom given to him (Peter the apostle and disciple) said that there will be a new heaven and a new earth where no 'something' dwells/remains. Check it out, woman! (I'm fucking about today; I need to get my arse in gear! FOCUS!)

(From 2 Peter 3:11-14) Peter said, 'Seeing then that things shall be dissolved and time is running out for this world, you can ask yourself what kind of person are you? Are you the sort of person the Lord is looking out for? As the days are rushing on to the coming of the Day of God (that day is upon us now, at this time; He is speaking to you all, He has lifted Himself up, making Himself clear): The day of God, wherein the heavens eventually being on fire, shall be dissolved and the elements shall melt with fervent heat (this will happen eventually, as I have already explained). Nevertheless we, according to His promise, look for new heavens and a new earth, where only the right things (righteousness) dwells or lives. Therefore beloved (well loved), seeing that you look for such things, be diligent that you may be found of Him in peace.'

Peter goes on to show that the Lord has been waiting and taking His time before He returns, giving more people the opportunity to change their minds, to believe Him. Both Pater, (I meant Peter but perhaps Pater is also correct, I must include the Father; pater means father in Latin, I think); Peter and

Paul appreciated that some things are hard to understand (without the help and guidance of the Holy Spirit) for those that are uneducated in the ways of God. Some have tried to find out the truth and many differences of opinion have arisen and much of the time they tie themselves and others in knots and even destroy lives with the dogmatism and arrogance of their beliefs. They make heavy burdens for people to carry, punishing, unattainable rules to follow. This is *not* His way. On a more individual level if we are not open to or accepting of the real truth and pushing Him away, we begin to doubt the Lord's love and care and then we can very easily get in a state and go mad with all the worry and doubts and fears, which replace the genuine, deep seated confidence only believing in Him can give.

The word Peter uses for this mindset is *unstable.* The opposite of being unstable is having the strength of character and resolve to trust in God. He has promised to vindicate and uphold His will/His ultimate plan for mankind; for all those who love Him. Peter's advice is simple: don't worry about what you do not understand, weigh up the understanding that is being given and consider whether it rings true or makes any sense or if it alternately puts any undue pressure on you to conform to man's ideals or control. 'Grow in His grace' and kindness and in the true knowledge and understanding about our Lord Jesus Christ. We will thank Him for ever for the liberty He brought, the freedom, from any form of bondage or restriction or law, which He has provided. (If you are into bondage for kicks and that is your thing then carry on, provided it is between consenting adults, but it's a 'grey' area (several shades of, apparently!). God hasn't got a problem with that. It is a slippery slope though because, as with anything that becomes obsessive, it can become all consuming and bondage can become cruel in extreme, so take care.)

Getting back on track to Matthew 12:37 and he unclean spirits who deliberately keep people in cruel bondage; this reference begins when Jesus said that we will be justified or condemned by our words; by the choice we make. Are you *unstable* (as is the Devil) or are you for the truth? The mouth speaks (see v35) ultimately what is in the heart... *except* in the case of some people with Tourette's! (and other similar conditions). We all have thoughts which we do not like to accept are from our heart, but we all do have corrupt thoughts, especially when we do not like someone or they irritate us. But it is offensive only to God when we try to hide it and pretend we are all holy and lovely and never dislike anyone. This festers and the whole being or personality becomes rotten. (There are people that I love but I do not like them and there are others that I like to a certain extent but I struggle to love them, usually because I do not quite trust them; sometimes they surprise me if I wait but there are some that never quite cut it for me. Others I am completely cold to; I feel nothing, neither love nor hate... nothing. The main thing is I am honest with the Lord about it and I remain open minded because He can and does surprise me. But I rarely let my guard completely down or take my armour off.)

One guy with Tourette's on the TV prog was chucking out all kinds of insults and kept apologising and insisting that they did not reflect how he really felt or was thinking. This is what persuaded me that this was the cruel work of unclean spirits/devils. Poor bloke; it is a most unkind and frustrating affliction.

This is what the Lord, Jesus, went on to say about evil spirits: they come and go but without proper intervention from the Lord they will always return and every time they come back the affliction gets worse. I must insist that in 99% of the cases of people with Tourette's etc. the individuals concerned HAVE NOT done anything to ask for this, they have not invited these spirits in; unclean spirits do not need an invitation, they are just prowling around looking for the vulnerable.

In a sense it is a sign, as these things are among us (and this is prophesied as a sign that the End days are upon us), that the Devil himself is also visibly at work. Not very subtly in this case but more to the point he is sowing wicked seeds/wicked thoughts against God and against good people, in the hearts of some men and women and children and making people think He doesn't care. If we entertain or follow these thoughts and allow ourselves to become poisoned, eventually we would be rotten through and through (as I said earlier); to the very core and loving it; (see Luke 8:12 the Parable of the Sower) the Devil comes and takes the good/the truth out of good hearts to prevent them from believing and being saved from death.

People with Tourette's generally hate the stuff they spew out, they do not like to be so very different and know they would be better off without it. If you suffer with Tourette's I would advise you to turn to Him and ask and He will make them leave you alone. No need to involve anyone else. Ask Him believing and He *will* do it. But you *have to* believe.

The following are scriptural/historical examples of individuals who were tormented in the same way while the Lord was on earth: Mary Magdalene: (Luke 8:2) it clearly states that seven devils had been removed or evicted from Mary and there were other women who were with Him, who had been healed of evil spirits and infirmities and they shared their food and such like with Him; they understandably loved Him very much.

A man called Legion: (Mark 5:1-20) This man was living in a cave and the poor guy was infected with an evil spirit who had multiple personalities, who tormented the man to an insane level. This was why he was called Legion, '*for we are many*'. He had all these different vile and unearthly worries and problems and all kinds of shit, tearing him apart; he had torn his clothes off and he was crying and cutting himself with sharp stones to try and stop the torment in his mind. Self harm, mutilation and cutting are not a modern phenomenon: self mutilation is satanically inspired, make no mistake. His aim is to defile and destroy the form that God created. People were afraid of Legion (his real name and personality was crowded out by these vile things) because he was also incredibly strong, it was impossible to restrain him as he simply snapped the chains. Jesus wasn't fazed, He just said, 'Come out of the man you unclean spirit' or words to that effect, 'get the fuck out' would do it! The moment He saw the demented man, He knew what was bothering him. That one spirit didn't even realise that he was only actually one personality, the spirit himself was in torment with a split personality. What a fucking mess. The Lord gave the spirit permission to go in to a herd of

2,000 pigs nearby and they ran violently over a cliff and drowned in the sea. The owners of the pigs went and told everyone in the local city what had happened and they came and found the man sitting fully clothed, in his right mind, but incredibly the people were more afraid and asked the man to leave the area (nice, isn't it? There is no accounting for the attitude of some people; no compassion; totally selfish, it beggars belief.)

Following this the man asked Jesus if he could stay with Him but the Lord told him to go home to his friends and tell them, publish, the great thing that the Lord had done for him and how He, Jesus and God, had shown the compassion that was lacking in the people of the city. All the men and women he told were amazed and hopefully thanked God for it. This is basically what the Lord has told me to do: publish my faith and life of faith; advertise Him.

The attitude of the Pharisees (strictly Jewish) and rulers was much the same as the people who had no compassion for the tormented man. (Matthew 12:22-32) When the Lord healed the blind and the deaf and cast out another devil, on another occasion, the Jewish leaders said that 'He cast out devils by Beelzebub (Satan) the prince of devils'. Ignoramus'; this is a clear example of not understanding the truth and having no desire to find it. They will be held accountable.

Jesus' reply was brilliant: 'Every kingdom divided against itself is brought to ruin. If Satan casts out Satan he is divided against himself', in other words 'don't be bloody stupid', what they were suggesting makes no sense; Jesus clearly wasn't working for Satan, who wouldn't want his workers cast out or evicted. The genuine eviction or removal of devils is of the Lord, with the help of the holy Spirit, and is final and it is another sign that the kingdom of God is with or upon us, 'the kingdom of God is come unto you'. Satan does use people to command his minions to leave but it's just an act; they just wander around for a while and then return with some of their mates and the poor soul that is being tormented is in a worst state than at the start.

God is gathering all His children together and in the process He will put Satan and his followers in chains, tie *them* up, and thoroughly restrain them. The Lord, Jesus, concluded by saying, in effect, 'Who is with me?' and brushed aside their nonsense. He made little of it.

The Lord will, He clearly says here, forgive anything else, but not insulting the Holy Spirit, saying He works for the Devil. As previously observed, the Lord called these leaders 'the generation of vipers', vicious snakes who speak with forked tongues! They didn't genuinely care for the people and didn't respect the Lord. Some ministers today pretend to be good, that they know and love God, but they are evil through and through, they have no real love for God or knowledge or understanding of the truth. Their words and actions show it.

Finally, we have the example of King Saul of Israel, who most probably was inflicted with a form of Tourette's or something very similar, later in his life (1 Samuel 16:14-23). Originally King Saul, the man chosen by the people to be their king, was blessed by God but he rejected/ignored the Lord's advice and therefore the Lord rejected him from being king.

Saul listened to what the people had to say and what they wanted rather than listening to the Lord and respecting His will. (He was another men' pleaser, see chapter 15 for details). It was very sad, and in fact Samuel, who was the prophet of the Lord at that time and the king's spiritual advisor, 'cried to the Lord all night' but it was made clear that Saul had become arrogant and vain, and he hadn't done what was necessary for the tribe of Israel to succeed. (The opposing tribes and their possessions should have been completely eradicated.) This might surprise some of you, who would not expect the Lord to be so brutal but the Lord knew what He was doing. Eventually the enemy tribes that weren't eradicated, were used to introduce idolatry and various practices, which robbed them of their land and so much more. Israel today is testament to that. The evidence is there for all to see; nothing has changed, even though the Lord Himself came here, as Jesus, to show them another way. Their stubbornness has got them nowhere. Saul put the whole future of Israel in jeopardy by ignoring some of Jehovah's instructions. There were many battles over land and territory during that period (as there is today, of course). The Lord advised or instructed Samuel to anoint a shepherd lad called David to be king in Saul's place. David was only a youth but he was strong, a tough bugger, both physically and in his trust in the Lord/Jehovah. He killed a giant called Goliath with a sling and stones (giants were the offspring of the sons of God, who sided with Satan and had sex with women on earth), and David killed a lion and a bear, who attacked his flock. He was a good man too.

From the time of David's anointing to be king the Spirit of

the Lord left or departed from Saul and (this is unusual) 'an evil spirit *from the Lord* troubled (terrified) him'.

This is not a regular thing. Saul had a tremendous responsibility, as king, and he knew this and the Lord was understandably angry, He was livid with Saul. God does get angry sometimes, same as we do. Samuel (who was not a violent man) had to put right Saul's mistake and finish off the king of the tribe who would have destroyed Israel, by hacking him to pieces). Saul's servants realised that an evil spirit was terrifying him and advised him to find a man who could play the harp, recognising that the music would soothe him and lessen the affects. Interestingly, it was David who was called for (Saul was unaware that he had be chosen to be king in his place; the changeover was not immediate). While David played on the harp, the evil spirit left Saul alone and he was refreshed. This is the bare bones of a small part of this interesting and intriguing period in Israel's history. The point is that clearly music does have a powerfully therapeutic purpose in the control of the effects of evil spirits.

However, these unclean, wicked spirits and these spirits are beings, sons/angels, who fell and gave up their heavenly forms. The word/Bible also speaks of Cherubims and Seraphims, other heavenly beings, who have a different form and purpose of their' own. The fallen sons can take on other forms; they can inhabit a physical human body. The sons and angels who remain can appear in human form; they might already look like humans but they have the ability to travel through the different dimensions. These wicked spirits/souls crave water and rest (they walk in a dry land Luke 11:24), they are lost without a body and this is why they take possession of human bodies that are not their own. But they are squatters and can be eradicated and kicked out forever by God.

As I explained, in the majority of cases the Lord is not condoning or agreeing with the behaviour of these evil spirits and He rarely uses them to exert or establish His authority. It is only in extreme cases. I advise any of you who are being tormented, to ask for deliverance and healing. There is nothing to fear or be afraid of, it is unlikely that any of you who are still reading this deserve this kind of punishment. This is what it is, Satan punishing people for being vulnerable and good, except, as I have explained, very, very occasionally people do deserve it and in this case the person involved would have been warned and therefore know the reason why, probably several times, beforehand. I hesitated to write these things because I want to avoid seeming to suggest that half the population is 'possessed'; this is for those who are severely tormented or afflicted in the same or similar manner as the examples I have given.

Another example of this nature is found in the New Testament (1 Timothy 1): the apostle Paul wrote to his great friend Timothy (Paul was his guide and mentor and called Timothy his son, as he loved him so much for his faith) and in the course of the letter he explained that he had handed two guys who had been causing trouble and division over to Satan. Paul tells us that they needed to learn not to blaspheme, which means to tell harmful tales, spread lies, basically talking about individuals behind their back and undermining the truth about God. (Calumnious [lying] against God and men; I had to include that because it is another unusual word that I have just learned from word of the day in the dictionary, which I like.) This problem was obviously beyond Paul, he had attempted to settle things but there was nothing else left for him to do. They had evidently pissed him off big time. Paul wouldn't do this lightly.

One of my reasons for telling you this is that the two who were made an example of were called Hymenaeus and Alexander. The man who abused me and my friends and deceived us, misinformed us for his own sexual gratification, was called Alexander and the Lord drew our attention to the fact that Alexander means the cock. He is a prick, that is for certain and I am also assured by the Lord that he has also been handed over for Satan to do his worst. Also it cannot be coincidence that Hymen' and the Cock are united in this instance. They are an insult to their namesakes and not deserving of them. They (and the pile-of-crap prick that we knew) degraded a most beautiful God given union and pleasure. Furthermore we were raped/robbed of our spiritual innocence. Whether the Alexander that I was unfortunate enough to be associated with will be able to recognise that he was wrong is doubtful (he is far too vain and arrogant and stubborn). If he can't see that he was deceived then he absolutely deserves everything that is coming to him. I have no more grace or feeling for him and as far as I am aware the Lord no longer cares, so if he can find it in himself to change his mind, he is going to have to beg. If you have had any experience of bullying or abuse then you will understand. The Lord is fair. This man allowed himself to be deceived to an extreme; honed in on our weakness and catered to his own lusts and almost destroyed this little flock. All that remains is little more than a handful of us and we all bear the scars. (The sad thing is, he had it right in the beginning, but he went the way of the devil, who also fell from a great height.

(17th September 2012) I trust that I have successfully outlined some of the truths and dispelled some of the myths about what is good and of God and what is Satan's work. Clearly one of the messages that is loud and clear is that abuse of another human being (or animals for that matter), deliberately causing physical or emotional pain, is not acceptable and God takes it very personally because we were made by Him, we are His children, His sons and daughters; we are like Him. It is morally unacceptable and Paul advised Timothy, who knew the truth (and I also take his advice on board), to stand firm in our confidence and belief in the truth about God, as an example of what is acceptable.

Hymeneaus and Alexander were examples of the type of people that we still see today, who destroy precious lives (what they do is as final and destructive as 'a ship wreck' or in our language 'a train wreck or a fatal car crash'). The Lord detests bullies, controlling arrogant bullies, more than anything else on this earth... and by way of redress, to put things right on behalf of those who suffer largely in silence, to make things equal He sets Satan/the devil himself on the offenders in extreme cases so they know what it is like to be oppressed by someone stronger and much more powerful than themselves.

The final subject that I need to speak about here (as this is the end days and this other emotive subject and life choice is another factor of these times) is vegetarianism and veganism.

I will discuss this subject but I'm looking forward to moving on from this chapter, to share some good news... this world is in such unnecessary bondage because of myths and 'old wives' tales' (which is basically what religions are), and some 'new wives' tales' (they are being added to as we breathe), they can rule our everyday lives and disturb our peace, many have been killed and others have killed themselves in the process, believing they are doing God's work, because of erroneous, misguided teaching. They are suffocating us! Christ Jesus came here 2,000 years ago to free us from these limitations. The majority of people know of Him and yet they choose to believe lies, they cannot see what He came for or what He achieved, for us... FOR US. It grieves me immensely. I am compelled to speak up.

Calm yourself Jayne! Take a deep breath. All is well. He is here. The holy Spirit will bless this work, my labour. It is time to publish the truth and free the innocent prisoners. If you want it, if you can believe and hear it: 'Hear Him', as the Father Himself advised; do you recognise His voice?

(1 Timothy 3:16)

'Without controversy (we cannot argue with this) *great* is the mystery of godliness' (what is good). It is a massive subject and there is much to understand but, basically, what has happened is 'God (in the form or person of Jesus) was manifest or appeared, was shown, in the flesh (He came as a man; a real living, feeling, breathing man), He was justified in the spirit, in the spirit he displayed (He proved He had the right character and morals and conscience of God; He had the mind of God in that He showed God, His Father, as a compassionate and caring and loving and patient and tolerant and just being; He was not afraid to stand up to the bullies and reprobates); He was seen of angels (angels in the form of good people on earth and in the form of heavenly angels/beings were witnesses to this, and this continues even to this day); He has been preached/taught/declared around the world (to Jews and gentiles ie everyone else alike) and He was, while He was here, believed on by some in the world and then He was received up to glory. He is now in a glorious and wonderful place and He has provided a way for us to join Him'.

This is the simple truth. This is all that we actually need to know but man has made it complicated by complicating our lives and creating misunderstandings about who God really is. I know there will be some who have come into contact with me that will feel that I have disturbed the peace but the existing peace for many is shallow and temporary and very fragile and not real. There will also be others who cannot see a problem. Sometimes when things are in knot it is necessary to make the mess worse in order to straighten things out. Do not take my word for it, judge for your selves, examine yourselves with the truth that I have been enabled to show in the true light. I advise only that you determine for yourselves whether this will help you in this life and the next; whether I am speaking the truth. Clearly there are some who do not need this advice; your lives are sorted, you already live in true peace, even though you are not outwardly 'Christian'; you have the basic, simplistic love for the truth and for Him already bound firmly in your hearts and in your lives. Praise Him if that is the case; praise God, praise His son, Jesus Christ, this is all He wants from us.

Don't change or alter yourselves, you are perfect exactly as you are.

Non-meat-eaters take heed, listen, because this next bit is especially for you:

One of the ways that Satan /the enemy has deceived some people and diverted them from the simplicity of God's way is to persuade people that it is wrong to eat animal flesh/meat. (1Timothy 4:1-7) 'Now the Spirit is outspoken about this particular subject: in the latter times, the End days, some will depart from the faith (the true way of God) listening to seducing spirits and doctrines/teachings of devils (*the* Liar); speaking lies in hypocrisy (they are often hypocritical); having their conscience seared with a hot iron....' These beliefs are burned into their conscience. Not eating meat, abstaining from meat and meat products becomes all consuming to religious proportions. In the majority of cases they will not open their mind to accept that they are mistaken or wrong. In actual fact it is in most cases a vanity, which goes against man's natural nutritional requirements and needs and we have the ability to chew and extract the nutrients from and digest meat, eaten in moderation. Additional to this are the spiritual implications. This 'doctrine' is another ploy or method of the enemy to distract mankind from God's ways and away from what is acceptable before God, in His sight and singling them out, separating them from society as a whole; it is another 'religion'. We need the nutrients in meat and none meat eaters do pay even if they have supplements. They only occasionally try and force their beliefs on others and they are not harming anyone else but they are being deceived and robbing themselves. (If you dislike the flavour of some meats or it is affecting your health that is an entirely different matter, please be clear on this.)

Peter continues to say, '...forbidding to marry (this must have been a feature in Peter's time, I do not see how this applies today, but I have not studied this closely; perhaps it makes you less horny, I don't know) and commanding (demanding they are right) to abstain from meats (food, so this includes any natural food fad not only animals), which God created to be received with thanksgiving by those who are educated about the truth'. The truth is, in this case, that this was simply God's original way of providing and preserving fresh food. He made animals before there were such things as freezers and fridges and even vegetables and fruit are designed by Him to have a reasonable shelf life and we could thank Him, for His ingenuity and thoughtfulness. It is understandable that some people might not like the flavour of certain foods and in these days of preservatives and food supplements and such like, people do have a choice. But, do not be persuaded that it is *wrong* to eat anything (as long as it is not poisonous or infected or rotten) that tastes nice.

'Every creature of God is good, and nothing to be refused, if you have a clear conscience, if you can accept that this is true.' In some circumstances of extreme famine, for example, even the things that would normally be considered poisonous could be eaten provided we ask the Lord for His protection; the body is very adaptable.

I hesitated to share this with you and explain it because I am tired and find these subjects frustrating and narrow minded and the enemy is to blame, so I am annoyed with him really. But Paul concludes by saying, 'If you put people in remembrance of these things (if I tell you about it), I will be a good minister of Jesus Christ, fed with and educated in the words of faith and truth, this is the food, the spiritual nourishment that really matters/counts in the long term.' As I have said, so many times, I know the truth about God and good teaching and I have to speak up on His behalf, for your sakes. He wants you to have a richer life, both here and in eternity. No one who has read this book can say that that they weren't well informed. I have an inspired responsibility to give you the facts, to kick out and supersede the garbage and old wives tales and the misconceptions, which are more widely taught and replace it with the God' honest truth. However, Proverbs 15:17: 'Better is a dinner of herbs where love is, than a fat ox where hatred is.' This is the bottom line. Personally, I would rather eat veg and herbs in a home full of love than have anything and everything I desire and live in a house full of hate - and the Lord agrees.

Amen and good night to this chapter: So be it, over to you, you makes your choice: freedom or bondage? The choice is yours. I apologise for sounding so weary, but I am, just for the moment. This has been a tough chapter because I have had to give so much of my time to speaking about the Enemy but it is necessary to know one's enemies as well as one's mates.

Clearly I need a break. I am not pissed off with you; I am annoyed with the blasted enemy (as usual). I should not allow him and his ways to rattle my peace.

I would rather speak about the Lord. I love the Word of truth; I just scrolled down to the last verse of this chapter and find the Lord Himself ended this chapter by saying to me, 'Look after yourself, and the teaching: continue as you have been doing and you will save both yourself and those that hear.' This is what *I* need to hear. Amen and Amen again to that; or, as a little girl I know so rightly said, 'Aaah men!' God Bless you all who hear.

To conclude this chapter (Luke 11:28) 'Happy are they who hear the word of God and let it grow in their heart'.

Most people crave peace and happiness and hearing God (our Father, Jesus our Lord, or the holy Spirit) is the only way to find real happiness and keep it forever.

The only sign that counts, that confirms that all this is true is (from v29) the sign of the prophet Jonah (Jonas), who was in the belly of the whale for three days, until it spat him out. Jesus Himself was in the belly of hell for three days and He came back from there to show the way for us. If you can believe only this, your every desire and more will be yours for all eternity. Jesus/the Lord was and is the greatest prophet and these are His words, His promise. Jonah means Dove and doves are recognised by God for the warmth of their mating. (I rest my case for fantastic, warm, loving, passionate sex for those who crave it, in the new earth and in our heaven)

CHAPTER 14

(15th Sept 2012) Tonight I have to break my own routine, which is not a rule but simply a habit, which feels as if it is going to be difficult because I have been to the local (pub, definitely is a pub and cannot be classed as a bar; it is a proper village pub and the hub of the community). The landlords of this particular establishment are not local but outsiders who, like me, hope to make enough money to move on to a 'better' life (in the sun) and nothing wrong with that; the climate here is shit, no two ways about it. But I can guarantee they, like me, will miss the warmth and stoicism of the locals and their pride in their family and community. I will miss all the new friends I have met everywhere I have stayed in the last two years, from each community, and some from my previous life. I wish you all nothing but the best from Him.

Thankfully, we do all have a better community and country to come in eternity and I trust that many of the people whom I have had the pleasure of sharing my life with (however briefly) will be at the heart of His and our family in heaven, or on the new earth.

I have found more genuine love in the pubs than in many

churches, where there appears to be more fakes and pretenders/actors, seeking to impress the vicar or priest or minister or rabbi or whoever is in charge, more than God. That is certainly true of the 'Christian' churches/religions, although I do appreciate that there are some congregations who , in this modern day, are in touch with God. I cannot judge at this present time regarding other religions. They certainly appear to have more zeal for God, even though it is also misguided. The point from the beginning of this book, bears repeating however; there are good people everywhere, who believe in God, and He is calling you all, using this mobile.

I have to take the opportunity, to tell you what I have learned because now I see how blessed I am. My world is spinning (not my head) because, although I had intended to only go out for a short while and have a quick drink, hours have passed, and several drinks have also passed... through my lips and I have had the pleasure of companionship with people I have grown to love; the holy Spirit Himself is set on fire with joy and happiness within me. This village has surprised me beyond all expectation. They are a motley crew, a diverse bunch, a small sample and an example of the people to be found in the world at large, but there are one or two very special individuals who, as in all societies, are constantly trying to assert their deep moral conviction, to convince others that they are basically good, kind, people. There are some who are waiting for an authoritative word of assurance to support their conviction, a word that rings true and speaks to their heart, their soul. You will remember Col; he is the lovely guy who inspired the title for the book. I have nothing to add, except to say that he has made his mark, his name is written in heaven, his place is secure. He asked me tonight if he would be surprised by the contents of the book; would he see a side to me that he did not already know? I was able to say, without hesitation, he would for certain and that this is a book that is absolutely for both men and women alike. I know he is hoping that there will be some sex... well my new friend, if you have stuck with it so far, I can only say that within the pages of this book there is a very strong promise of good sex to come in heaven. Your every desire will be fulfilled and more. You are a good man, through and through. You are an example of the good people whom He has noticed and is watching over, who do not even realise it. What more do I need to say? Except... God bless and be happy with your lovely wife. (I want to say too that God isn't watching us all the time, in the sense of spying on us; He is just checking in occasionally to see how we are doing and looking out for genuine people.)

The biggest surprise for me in my present home village has been the people that I couldn't see the first time I came here. I wouldn't have missed you all for the world. Thank you. I guess that is how the Lord feels about His first visit to Earth. Then He came mainly to the Jews, except for the odd exception, like the woman of Samaria (see John 4), who herself was a sign or example of the grace to come for the world. When He comes, in person, this next time it will be to recover all who have been looking for Him, and some He has only just this last hour been re-introduced to.

20th September 2012: Does anyone really want to stay in this temporary and deteriorating abode/home of a body that we currently reside in? We cannot patch it up and fix it indefinitely. Eventually it is going to pack in, wear out. We can only prolong the agony, through fear that this really is the only life we have. My vote is firmly in the everlasting life camp, with new bodies and minds that are indestructible and treasures of joy and peace and love beyond our wildest dreams and fantasies. 'That will do nicely thank you Lord. How kind and accommodating you are'. It's true!

21st September 2012 – All the signs are pointing to a possible visit to Australia for me next June or some time later. It's not the change I was expecting but the change I was anticipating has been put on hold for a while longer, so Australia sounds like a good place to wait: maybe get a break from the madness. The names of the lodge that we might be staying in and the suburb where it's located, both contain references to being sustained; fed and watered basically. I am going to be looked after by the Holy Spirit and the locals. There is double reference to a drought, which might mean a spiritual drought, but that is unlikely because the Spirit is going to keep me well fed in that respect, so maybe Oz is in for an especially dry season. We will see. There is another little surprise hidden in there, which is for me something to look forward to relating to the change that I have been promised. (It transpired that this accommodation was out of the question but nevertheless the Lord used it to give me a message; that still stands. So, things are starting to look good. I am coming to the end of another chapter and the beginning of another, in my life on earth and with Him, my Wonderful Friend and our heavenly Father. I call Him Wonderful because that is one of His names (Isaiah 9:6 'He shall be called Wonderful', which means a miracle, great and accomplished, and .... 'The Prince of Peace', and to my surprise, as I have never considered checking out the meaning of this before, it means He is the head person, the top man, to be happy, friendly, safe and well, to be at peace and make complete. This is Him and when He says we can be at peace this is what He is giving us, if we can accept it. Hello Mr Wonderful... He really is.

In my notebook this morning I wrote, 'I am me, I am simply myself. I am many colours, I am free ('together nothing can stop us now, there's no limit to what we have found'; I didn't write this, its playing on the radio as I type [Connor Maynard])... I am blah blah blah, I am tired, bloody tired of this life.' My Wonderful friend made me laugh out loud...speaking through the Radio: 'No one said it was easy!' Ha ha ha, very funny! But then I realised He is here, He is with me wherever I am and that is all that matters. He is here, in me, surrounding me, loving me. What more could I desire? Radio: 'Love taught me to fly; my Love taught me to cry/lie: it's not over'. It's *not* over 'till it's over', so I can be fairly certain He's not coming for us today.

27th October 2012: Today is a good day (fanfare!) This is my life. This morning I accepted that I have a life, which might seem like an odd thing to say, as this is what I keep saying to you guys. Nothing tangible has changed. I am still awaiting the fulfilment of what I consider to be His important promises to me, which will improve my life in this life considerably, but the difference is I can wait. I am content. I am confident in His arms. I have almost stopped smoking, I am not scared of the laptop anymore; it is only a machine, my brain is surely more advanced than a computer... no really, it is... I can shut it down and survive without it!

I trust God, my Father and the Lord, my friend and Brother, Mr Wonderful. This is my life and it is a wonderful life, full of hope and peace in my heart. What more could I ask. I have my marbles (a sound message for my Grandson, I am sure he will be delighted, as he keeps asking me when and how I lost my marbles, darling boy). I am not conventional; I am unpredictable and volatile but then so is God. I love His children and I have experienced His kindness from those who are like Him. Thank you to anyone who has helped me or come to my aid along the way (A message for Sarah here, I am very sorry I never thought to take your full name but I am certain I will see you again, one day soon). He is faithful, this is what really counts in this life. Creed is playing on the mp3: 'Life has just begun; are you ready for Us to come?' Perfect timing...as always! I wouldn't expect anything less. Momentarily I wondered about His promises and the radio in the next room gave me confidence, 'trust me babe, believe in me; I ain't lying'. How could I ever doubt Him?

My life still looks like a complete shambles but we know better. I haven't even begun to share my memories from my journals (especially my travels with Him in Europe) but then perhaps they are mine. They are for me to know and for you to wonder! It is time for you to find your life with Him; time to listen to and look for your own signs, His message to you, my friends, His friends and sons and daughters. There is nothing to fear. There is only life and light and peace and happiness and joy to come with Him. No one is saying it will be easy immediately and it is not over yet but now you have hope and a guaranteed (such is my confidence!) promise of incredible, amazing things to come with Our heavenly Father and His Spirit and His firstborn Son, the Wonderful Prince of Peace.

The conclusion of the matter is that we are what we are, this is what God intended and this is not The End; it is the Beginning... the beginning of Life... everlasting; the beginning of a tremendous adventure. Praise Them! Soon be time to PARTY!

Look Up! He is gathering you in; Maranatha guys: He is coming!

EPILOGUE

I have just had the most unexpected and beauuudiful day (this one is for you Col and Ange; his guardian Angel). This is the hardest part to type because I feel I am stretched too far but

I know that I do not have to raise my voice to be heard because you, dear Reader, are home and dry. I have no concern because you will have the most wonderful surprise. It is not a puzzle or a riddle and perhaps not the surprise you expected but all will be made clear: You will see Him when He comes and everything else will be forgotten in the glory of that moment, in the blink of the eye. God bless you my friends. See you .... whenever!

The question for me now on this earth is, will those who are closest to me and Him and those who share in this understanding of His will and plan for mankind, in these end days, will they hold fast to their faith, will they reject me now this book is in print? Can they believe this is His will? I guess they too have done what they could!

Another question is, Where do I go from here, Lord and Father? Will you answer my requests? and Will you vindicate my faith, my trust in you? But then, I know the answer and I do not need to see what my ultimate heaven entails and holds for me because I know it will be bloody good... and that's good enough for me. Cheers Father; cheers Lord; Chow, Holy Spirit.

2/11/12: Ezekiel 8:4 The glory of the God of Israel was there, (Leviticus 3:17) It (the book, which is accepted as a sacrifice that is well pleasing to God) shall be a perpetual statute for your generations.

Jeremiah 31:4 I will be built again and I will dance again with those who make merry. Shout among the nations, publish ye. I am redeemed from the hand of him that was stronger than me.

He has heard my requests.

Praise Them!

Additional acknowledgments

2nd October 12: I would like to thank Sarah for noticing that I was in distress even before I fainted and cracked my head. And her pregnant friend who kindly massaged my leg (I want to call you Lee but I cannot be certain; I remember your face and trust that you have beautiful, perfect twins); and Peter for your coat to keep me warm. True Samaritans indeed. Your rewards will be great. And thank you Steve for loaning me your 'phone; I must say, I admire your persistent fishing skills, lol. If we haven't had that glass of wine it is because it was not meant to be. I trust you will find your own particular joy. And last but not least, thank you Babsi ...and Roland...and Yuki... and so many others: I will love you forever and long to see you again, in His perfect time. God bless you as always.

Thank you Hannah for your understanding and support; I know it's your job but I nevertheless appreciate your kindness and dedication. They have not gone unnoticed.

Thank you Patti for unwittingly/inadvertently providing me with a bolt hole, an occasional refuge, a haven, when my foot was broken; a place to escape from my own personal prison to wait on the Lord... your perfect reward is with Him.

POSTSCRIPT

During the course of the previous couple of years or more, He has taught me how to play the game and system of the world, through very real and sometimes bitter experience, in the good and the bad. Nothing of what I have endured is bullshit. He is the master of all things and the Master at playing or manipulating any system. The World and all it's ways are temporary but His world is everlasting.

3/11/12 Today is my daughter's birthday... Happy Birthday gorgeous; Happy Birthday. Tonight, this morning rather 3:15, I saw a slug scaling the heights—- you will be pleased to know there are 'slugs' in heaven (not literal slugs!). Thank fuck for that! Pc (or poor?) the decision is yours, Reader. Thank you Lord for accepting the slugs of this world, the despised of this life; Praise, praise, praise You!

13/11/12 My foot was broken in a freak accident (on the 9th) and I passed out and smacked my head on the concrete. Lovely kind Sarah and her friend and Peter came to my rescue (and Steve with his 'phone). It is only today that I saw the sign and heard the full message from Them (God) to me from that day (and what an annoying price to pay to get this message): 'It's alright love, there are good hearts out there, who want to hear what I have to say today!' Cheers my friends, cheers

Wonderful! Looking forward to toasting the Father and the Son whilst we all share some of the new wine in heaven.

Playing on the radio: 'You can find me somewhere down the crazy river (by Robbie Robertson)... I'm a (woman) with a clear destination...there's something you've got to learn, not to be afraid of it... but you will learn to love it!' Amen and Amen... So be it!

God's witness is everywhere, not only in the Bible. His ways and messages are tied up in history. You can hear them if you so choose. For me one of the most comforting messages is that the key to eternal happiness is to look up. It's not complicated. His provision and true reward for me comes from above and yours can be too. Why not let *the* Man worthy of any real distinction lead you there; to a new life and His great celebration.

It is mankind and the devil who have complicated God's simple life plan because men and women, and children, are so easily led (but to an extent our path is written in our genes and in our minds). We are not alone; He wants us to ask Him for His help to overcome the things which so easily weigh us down. This choice is yours.

I actually saw the stairway to heaven on that first night that He spoke to me. I was completely straight; no drugs or drink in me, but I saw the sky light up in a multitude of colours; the clouds parted and the sweeping stairway appeared. I know He is real.

The way of God is a bag of endless hidden treasures indeed. You might be wondering about 10th December 12; that was the day I got my peace back. He took me down a trip down Memory Lane, to places I have been, things I have seen over the centuries: all as true and vivid as this life. I can assure you He is real and I know my place and a hint of yours too.

12/12/12: Another significant day in His calendar; a message for me to confirm He is working; 12,12,12 a perfect number spiritually x3; perfection on perfection. I can't argue with that; I don't want to. 1, 2; 1, 2; 1, 2; sound check! sound check for what? God only knows, thankfully. History in the making or maybe hope for the future? Thankfully He never stops talking but I must as my work is done here. Bye for now and God Bless!

'Did her three wishes (hopes, requests) come true?' some of you might be wondering. The short answer is 'No...not yet!' However, I still believe in love. I was never a girl who believed in princesses and wishes coming true but now... I do.

www.ingramcontent.com/pod-product-compliance
Lightning Source LLC
LaVergne TN
LVHW051501080426
835509LV00017B/1852